CW00524089

The Sporting Art of
CECIL ALDIN

Aldin at work on a coaching picture in his studio at Purley, Berkshire.

THE SPORTING
ART OF
CECIL ALDIN

ROY HERON

· THE ·
SPORTSMAN'S
PRESS
LONDON

Published by
The Sportsman's Press 1990

© Roy Heron 1990

For Maureen, Ian and Sue

All rights reserved. No part of this publication may be
reproduced, stored in a retrieval system, or transmitted
in any form or by any means, electronic, mechanical
photocopying, recording or otherwise, without the prior
permission of the publishers.

British Library Cataloguing in Publication Data
Heron, Roy
The sporting art of Cecil Aldin
1. English graphic arts. Aldin, Cecil, 1870–1935
I. Title
760.092

ISBN 0-948253-50-9

Photoset and printed in Great Britain by
BAS Printers Limited, Over Wallop, Hampshire

CONTENTS

ACKNOWLEDGEMENTS

The author and publisher wish to thank everyone who has contributed to this book, either with information for the text or help with the illustrations. In particular they express their gratitude to Nicholas Potter of The Burlington Gallery, Angela Holder of Gallery Five, Peter Rose of Phillips, Anthony C. Mason, Mrs Peter Norman, Pat and Penry Archer, Colin Tucker, *The Illustrated London News*, the proprietors of *Punch*, and to the staffs of Sotheby's, Christie's, Spinks and Lawrence Fine Art of Crewkerne. The author's special thanks go to Melanie Graham for her photographic expertise. He owes a debt of gratitude to Mrs Kathleen Aldridge; to the late Denis Aldridge, who encouraged his interest in Aldin, and to Susan Coley, the editor of this volume.

A nod of acknowledgement must also go to the shade of R.S. Surtees, whose works – particularly *Handley Cross* – figured prominently in Cecil Aldin's life and whose words, through the mouth of Jorrocks, adorn each of our chapter headings.

LIST OF COLOUR PLATES

PLATE 1
John Gilpin, a little watercolour drawing completed when CA was eight years old and copied from Randolph Caldecott's book.

Caldecott's version of John Gilpin's ride, engraved and printed by Edmund Evans.

Three Jolly Huntsmen. An early Aldin print and another theme obviously inspired by Caldecott.

PLATE 2
Admiration. Among the first of CA's pictures in the style that was to make his name. Dated 1897, it was issued as a print by Louis Meyer.

Full Cry, from *The Fallowfield Hunt*, the set of six prints which became famous on both sides of the Atlantic.

PLATE 3
Cadbury's Cocoa. Among the best known of Aldin's posters, but not as forceful as his work for Colman's.

The Portsmouth Coach. Coaching featured in many Aldin prints.

PLATE 4
Lady Currie with her sons, Bill and Hamish, following the staghounds on Exmoor.

The Devon and Somerset crossing Badgworthy Water, Exmoor, in the 1920s.

PLATE 5
A Fall's a Hawful Thing. A pencil, ink and watercolour drawing for the Surtees classic, *Handley Cross*.

PLATE 6
Bunkered! From *Twelve Old English Sporting Pictures*.

Home. Also from the Sporting Pictures set.

PLATE 7
The Twelfth. Another of the Sporting Pictures.

'I declare I forgot the cap.' A plate from *The Posthumous Papers of The Pickwick Club.*

PLATE 8
'Out for a Jolly,' from a watercolour impression by Snaffles of CA in a South Berks point-to-point.

The Prince of Wales (Duke of Windsor) enjoying himself with The Pytchley.

PLATE 9
A Likely Spot. The parson and the boy who featured in many an Aldin print indulge in a little fishing.

The First Fence. An example of Aldin's rollicking depiction of hunting in the early nineteenth century.

PLATE 10
Preston Rawnsley of the Southwold, on Bluebird. A large pastel portrait presented to him in 1920.

PLATE 11
A Timber Topper with The Quorn. One of four *Hunting Types* issued as prints.

Not a Hunting Seat, illustrating the wrong way over timber.

PLATE 12
Galloping Across the Map. The Edinburgh Mail at full stretch.

Nell, a spaniel, retrieving a cock pheasant. Pastel drawing used in the book *A Dozen Dogs or So.*

Two Tortoiseshell Spaniels, a type CA described as 'the most picturesque' he had painted.

PLATE 13
The South Berks. Aldin was connected with the hunt for about thirty years and became its secretary and Master.

Mr Jorrocks and his hounds leave the kennels at the start of a hunting day. From *Jorrocks on 'Unting.*

PLATE 14

'And they charged at the danger, and the danger took toll.' A pastel study used as an illustration for *Right Royal*, John Masefield's narrative poem about a steeplechase.

The Winner's Enclosure. Another illustration from *Right Royal*: 'To lead in the winner while the bookmakers cheered.'

PLATE 15

Polo at Dunster. This pastel was used as a cover illustration for *English Life* magazine, 1924.

PLATE 16

The Grand National, The Canal Turn. One of a set of four scenes from the 1920 race.

PLATE 17

Quality. A show jumper being led away, proudly bearing a winner's rosette. One of four pastels from which a series of prints was made, the others being a hunter, polo pony and heavy horse.

A Meet at Le Touquet. Lithographic print. Aldin took his all-children's pony show to France in 1929, under the patronage of The Prince of Wales and with Lord Lonsdale as the show president.

Cracker the bull terrier and CA's favourite, performing his trick of
running through the horse's legs while exercising on Exmoor.

INTRODUCTION

It is fifty-five years since Cecil Aldin died and few are alive who knew him; fewer still who rode to hounds in his company or saw his perky figure hacking across Exmoor in high summer with his dogs, threatening the life and limb of themselves and their master as they scurried within inches of the horse's hooves. He was born almost exactly in the middle of Victoria's long reign and he lived to see the emergence of Adolf Hitler, though not the tyrant's downfall. In his day, Aldin's hunting pictures had been compared to the work of Leech and Alken, and later to G.D. Giles and Lionel Edwards; his posters to those of Hassall and Hardy; his ancient inns to Dendy Sadler's; his coaching scenes to the Wrights' and his children's book illustrations to Caldecott's, which was all very gratifying to Aldin and gave some indication of the range of this multi-talented man. In one other area he was beyond compare: the portraits of dogs, and particularly those which he made

A rapid sketch of CA by Lance Thackeray. The two were close friends and, in younger days, went on painting expeditions together to the hopfields of Kent.

towards the end of his life. This volume is concerned with his sporting art, which provided the bulk of his output and was his main source of income. As with everything he did, his sporting life and work was not confined to one aspect and went far beyond the hunting field to include racing, polo, coaching, coursing, shooting and even golf and cricket.

The 'lost years' of the Hitler war were largely responsible for Aldin's work being neglected, as he was unknown to the new post-war generation. My own interest in Aldin was awakened more than twenty years ago. I began several years of research, spurred on by his daughter, Gwen, and his grandchildren, Tony and Ann, and eventually published a biography and the first bibliography of his work. That book, long since out of print, opened the eyes of dealers and collectors, who realised Aldin had been vastly under-valued. As a result, pictures which could then be picked up for £30 or £40 now fetch thousands. No-one would be more pleased than his daughter at the attention and respect being paid once again to Aldin.

During research for this book I came across a little memoir which Gwen wrote and gave to me shortly before her death:

My Father – Cecil Aldin

'The earliest recollections I have of my father are set against the background of happy days in the nursery of our home in Bedford Park, Chiswick, where, with infinite patience, he guided the development of my brother, Dudley, and myself and responded to every notion that passed through our heads. We three all had red hair of the brightest hue, which may have intensified the bond between us.

'Each day we had a conspiratorial meeting after lunch, when father would tell stories and produce a surprise for us with all the panache of a conjuror. He gave us elementary riding instruction on wooden horses he had himself designed and made.

'Once, when telling a story, he painted directly on to the distempered wall a picture

How's That? Top-hatted cricket from
Twelve Old English Sporting Pictures (1901).

The Prince of Wales (Duke of Windsor) was an enthusiastic polo player and a bold horseman. He knew Aldin well, through their association in the hunting field.

of a cock being chased by a puppy. Every day after that he had, at our insistence, to add an animal, until the farmyard frieze encircled the room. I remember wearing a smock embroidered with rabbits copied from the frieze, when I was about three years old. The farmyard design later became familiar throughout Britain when it was used by a wallpaper manufacturer. From the pinto wooden horses, I graduated to a donkey called Jackie and, when I was six, an Exmoor pony. I rode the little Exmoor for several years, hacking and going to occasional hunts, on a leading rein. It was a great joy to be woken up early to go out with daddy on a cub-hunt when a meet was nearby. Having survived the somewhat painful experience of learning to jump, I was able to take part in gymkhanas and pony shows with Dudley. And always daddy was close at hand, encouraging, jesting and

A sportsman, his boy and pointers on a shooting expedition to the September stubble fields. Drawn in 1900 for *A Sporting Garland*.

Taking a stream, a drawing for one of the regular Hunting from London articles in *Land & Water Illustrated* (1904).

Gwen Aldin, aged twenty. She accompanied her father on many riding
holidays in the West Country.

cajoling us to greater efforts. He was an enchanting person. Children and grown-ups alike
adored his humour and genuine good nature.

'Dudley died at Vimy Ridge in the 1914–18 war, by which time I was helping my father
with his Remount Service duties, providing horses for the Army. Father and son were
very much alike and, had he lived, Dudley would have been a better than average artist.
We both, father and I, immersed ourselves in Remount work after Dudley's death. I was
part of the all-women staff at a depot with 300 horses in our care. This came about because
of the shortage of trained men. It was entirely Cecil Aldin's idea to advertise among hunting
families, where he knew many capable women looked after their own horses. The War
Office was sceptical but the response was beyond our wildest hopes and soon the idea
was copied by depots in other areas. I well remember Alfred Munnings coming to live

with us in 1915. He had lost an eye and was looking for some wartime job to do, preferably with horses. Munnings was young then, but the signs of genius were there and he shared daddy's studio. He was a great help because, besides being an expert horseman, he turned out to be an experienced treater of horses with mange.

'I took my father's favourite dogs out to his new home in Majorca when doctors advised him to live in a warm climate. After his death, I visited my mother on the island, expecting to find scenes of desolation and our villa in ruins, for the Spanish Civil War had just ended. But all was well. The only sign of the recent hostilities were the warships in the harbour and the uniformed soldiers who seemed to be everywhere.

'My mother lived on to her eighty-third year, when the name of Cecil Aldin, which in his lifetime was seen weekly in periodicals and several times a year on the covers of new books, had all but faded into history. The re-awakening of interest in his work would, of course, have given him enormous pleasure. All artists like to feel they are appreciated. I know my father would have been delighted, in particular, by the number of young people who have discovered and enjoyed his pictures and books, not least among them his great-granddaughter, Pat, too young to have known him but his most ardent fan and collector.'

Dudley Aldin as a 2nd Lieutenant in the Royal Engineers shortly before he was killed in action at Vimy Ridge in 1916.

A smooth fox terrier. Chalk drawing used as an illustration in *A Dozen Dogs Or So*.

I

NIMROD IN THE NURSERY

Bliss my 'eart, wot a many ways there is of enjoyin' the chase

The decline of sporting art in the second half of the nineteenth century was as mysterious as it was real. One by one, the giants of the early Victorian era were no more and for a time there was a lack of obvious candidates to take up the torch. Henry Alken's death in 1851 marked the beginning of the slide and further blows followed in the next decade. But the ten years which spanned the deaths of John Leech, J.F. Herring, James Pollard and Edwin Landseer saw the births of George Denholm Armour, Basil Nightingale, Frank Calderon and Cecil Aldin. Not far behind came Alfred Munnings, Lionel Edwards, Charlie Johnson Payne (Snaffles) and Charles Simpson. Those later years of Victoria and the whole of Edward's reign were among the most exciting times in which any artist could have grown to maturity. The laborious process of engraving by hand on wood and on metal gave way to new printing techniques which were used to marvellous effect in France, notably by Chéret, Toulouse-Lautrec and Mucha. The impact on any young artist visiting Paris in that era was tremendous.

The Frenchmen's mastery of the lithographer's art turned advertisements into pictures to be treasured, decorating the walls of the proudest homes as well as the streets. Broad areas of vibrant colour and confident black outlines replaced the meticulous – some would say dreary – style of the previous age. It was as if the young artists had been set free and their uninhibited work at first shocked and then enchanted Europe in a surging tide which soon reached London. Aldin was in his mid-twenties when first he went to Paris. He was intoxicated by the Bohemian atmosphere of the artists' quarter and the wealth of revolutionary ideas which permeated the whole city. He also fell in love with the French countryside and in subsequent years spent many happy hours touring by horse transport and bicycle around Normandy and Brittany, sketching the agricultural workers and their families in their smocks and wooden clogs, and following the staghounds, an experience which he used to full advantage in posters and illustrations for magazines and books. These helped to establish his reputation and provided the foundation on which he built his career as a sporting artist.

Although there was no tradition of hunting in his family, he had from childhood been fascinated by horses and dogs. Wellington Lodge, the house where Cecil Charles Windsor Aldin was born at Slough in 1870, has long since disappeared, the victim of a road-widening scheme. It was a substantial property, of a type occupied by people of some standing. When the Aldins lived there, it was part of a small community on the old coaching road to Bath, in no way resembling the place upon which John Betjeman wished friendly bombs to fall. Cecil had no recollections of the house, as the family moved when he was one year old and his first memories were of London. In his autobiography, with the sardonic title *Time I Was Dead*, he describes the awakening of his artistic interest in horses and dogs: 'My earliest remembrance of drawing from nature is that of a red-headed child sitting at a nursery window, high up in a Kensington home, waiting for tradesmen's carts to pull up at the back gate so that he could "dror" the ponies attached to them.' He went for walks in Kensington Gardens with his governess and, more often than not, they stopped at a toy shop, where Cecil took a fancy to wooden horses painted with large black spots. This childhood experience, he decided, accounted for his lifelong affection for odd-coloured horses. Among his first attempts at drawing were lively sketches of spotted horses throwing their riders and when, twenty or thirty years later, he made rocking horses for his two children and for the toy trade, the carved wooden models were in the same vein, being large, heavily spotted and very jolly.

Whether he knew it or not, Aldin's future was settled in the nursery. All around him were bound copies of *Punch* magazine and books containing illustrations by John Leech, Phiz (Hablot Knight Browne) and George Cruikshank. *The Graphic* and other periodicals taken by the Aldins regularly featured the work of leading sporting artists, including hunting and coaching engravings after Alken and Pollard, whose pictures also hung on the walls. The urge to 'dror' became irresistible as Cecil watched his father, a keen amateur artist, busy at the easel and was plied with pencils and paper to make his own pictures while sprawled on the floor. The novels of Charles Dickens, who died in the year Cecil Aldin was born, became firm favourites of his; and so did Anna Sewell's *Black Beauty*, which was published when Cecil was seven years old. But perhaps the greatest influence of those formative years was the publication of Randolph Caldecott's series of picture books, packed with gaiety and colour and depicting rollicking life in an idyllic countryside. One of the first of the books, *John Gilpin*, was given to Cecil at Christmas when he was eight. He was captivated and he copied the illustrations time and again. Each year he waited eagerly for Caldecott's next production and echoes from the books can be seen in much of Aldin's later work. The success of Caldecott's books owed much to Edmund Evans, whose engravings were ever faithful to the artists' intentions. (Joan Hassall, the eminent wood engraver, told me she was convinced Evans used a photographic method of placing the image on a block, ready for engraving, so close were the finished products to the original drawings.)

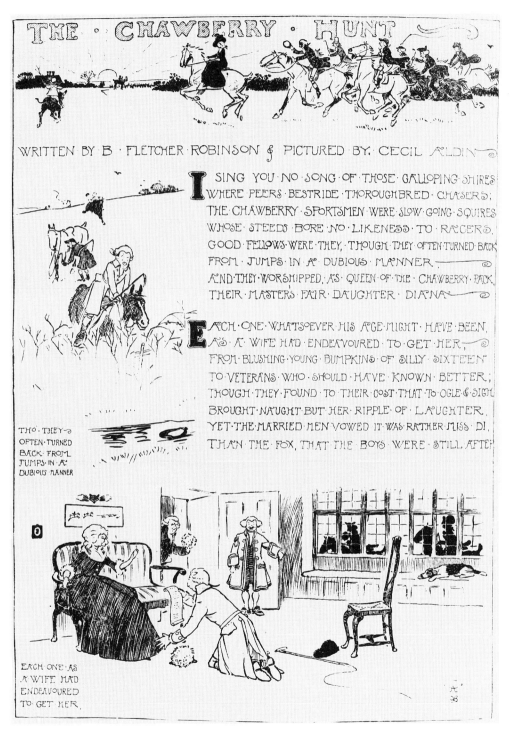

THE · CHAWBERRY · HUNT

WRITTEN · BY · B · FLETCHER · ROBINSON § PICTURED · BY · CECIL · ÆLDIN

I SING · YOU · NO · SONG · OF · THOSE · GALLOPING · SHIRES
WHERE · PEERS · BESTRIDE · THOROUGHBRED · CHASERS;
THE · CHAWBERRY · SPORTSMEN · WERE · SLOW · GOING · SQUIRES
WHOSE · STEEDS · BORE · NO · LIKENESS · TO · RACERS,
GOOD · FELLOWS · WERE · THEY, · THOUGH · THEY · OFTEN · TURNED · BACK
FROM · JUMPS · IN · A · DUBIOUS · MANNER
AND · THEY · WORSHIPPED, · AS · QUEEN · OF · THE · CHAWBERRY · PACK,
THEIR · MASTER'S · FAIR · DAUGHTER · DIANA

EACH · ONE · WHATSOEVER · HIS · AGE · MIGHT · HAVE · BEEN,
AS · A · WIFE · HAD · ENDEAVOURED · TO · GET · HER,
FROM · BLUSHING · YOUNG · BUMPKINS · OF · SILLY · SIXTEEN
TO · VETERANS · WHO · SHOULD · HAVE · KNOWN · BETTER;
THOUGH · THEY · FOUND · TO · THEIR · COST · THAT · TO · OGLE & SIGH
BROUGHT · NAUGHT · BUT · HER · RIPPLE · OF · LAUGHTER,
YET · THE · MARRIED · MEN · VOWED · IT · WAS · RATHER · MISS · DI,
THAN · THE · FOX, · THAT · THE · BOYS · WERE · STILL · AFTER

THO · THEY
OFTEN · TURNED
BACK · FROM
JUMPS · IN · A
DUBIOUS · MANNER

EACH · ONE · AS
A · WIFE · HAD
ENDEAVOURED
TO · GET · HER

The Chawberry Hunt. Pen and ink decorations for verses about slow-going hunting squires
by B. Fletcher Robinson, in the Christmas 1898 edition of *Cassell's Magazine.*

The Introduction. Hound puppies meet the hunters. On ivory paper heightened with body colour.

Aldin's art invariably has a sensitive touch about it and his genuine love for animals is apparent, so it understandable that all his life he felt deeply wounded by a childhood incident which led to him being branded unfairly as a sadist. The story has been told many times, but is worth repeating, in view of the effect on him. He and his two brothers, Arthur and Percy, had been transferred from Eastbourne College to Solihull Grammar School, because their parents were cutting down on expenses. Cecil, an introspective youth much given to lone walks in the Warwickshire countryside, rescued from a farm a mongrel puppy which was about to be put down. Against the rules, he took the animal back to school, where he kept it in a lavatory, feeding it daily on milk and scraps saved from the table.

Unfortunately, the puppy became ill and the older boys told Cecil the dog must be destroyed, as it was the kindest thing to do. Weeping copiously, he placed the struggling puppy into a bucket of water, with a lid on top. Soon all movement inside the bucket ceased. Just then, a bell summoned the boys to afternoon roll-call and Cecil hurried away, in the firm belief that his little friend was dead.

To his horror, a teacher found the puppy still alive, resulting in a stern lecture from the headmaster to the whole school, and to Cecil in particular, on cruelty to animals. Cecil cried himself to sleep for many a night after that and in 1934, only a year before his death, he wrote, 'I have never been able to drown even a kitten since that memorable occasion, and in my later life, although much of it has been in the hunting field, have always disliked seeing any hunted animal killed.' The headmaster, Dr Robert Wilson, was a wise man. He recognised the promise in his pupil's work and kept one of Aldin's first oil paintings, a horse's head painted on a wooden palette. And the school's old boys' association later elected him as their president. (Aldin's attitude to cruelty was emphasised in drawings which he made, showing the inhumane methods used by some animal trainers. Four of the drawings were used to illustrate a magazine article entitled 'The Torture of Trained Animals'. He also depicted a lost collie about to be taken into a laboratory, a drawing which the British Union for the Abolition of Vivisection issued as a postcard with the caption, 'A Stray Victim for the Vivisector'.)

When he reached the age of fifteen and the end of his schooldays approached, Cecil

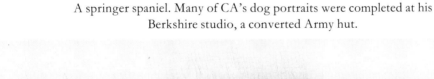

A springer spaniel. Many of CA's dog portraits were completed at his
Berkshire studio, a converted Army hut.

The Snail of the King's Highway. For more than a century this was the
country folks' omnibus and goods wagon, pulled by eight hairy-legged
heavy horses.

and his parents had numerous discussions about his future. Cecil, who had thus far shown no academic aptitude, had a fleeting ambition to become a coachman and marry his governess, after being impressed by the liveried splendour of the Lord Mayor of London's coachman. Mrs Aldin favoured the Church as a profession for her son, but her husband, impressed by Cecil's enthusiasm for art, had the final word and he was sent to the studio of Albert Moore, a painter in the classical mould, whose polished representations of domestic scenes in ancient Greece were to be seen each year at the Royal Academy exhibitions. Aldin stuck for a month the tedious exercises which Moore set his pupils: drawing a female head in charcoal, filling in the portrait with thick oil paint; scraping, sanding, then going over the whole in thin oils until the surface had the texture of a virgin ice rink.

His four weeks with Albert Moore helped Aldin not one step in his desire to be an animal artist and to hunt. He packed his paints, palettes and brushes and enrolled in the National Art Training School, which later became the Royal College of Art and which was within walking distance of his home. Aldin in later years poured scorn on his artistic efforts as a student. ('Like Mr Micawber I must have been a very great optimist, for my attempts at drawing animals in those youthful days showed no promise of ever being likely to earn even a living wage, and certainly never being able to provide me with horses to

Proud of 'er Brass, a heading for verses from *Scarlet, Blue and Green*
(1932).

A queer sort of fresh-painted vehicle. The Sheriff's
officer arrives for Mr Pickwick. From *Pickwick Papers*.

ride or hounds to hunt'.) Yet his fellow students – and they included the architect Edwin
Lutyens and the portraitists William Llewellyn and Richard Jack – were full of praise
for Aldin's work. His avowed intent was obvious in everything he did, for no matter
what subject he had been set, the paper or canvas would be framed by forceful line drawings
of horses and dogs. It was dogs which led to his first commission, from Miss Emily Moore,
who owned an ancient coaching inn at Leatherhead, in Surrey, a lovely building which,
alas, was demolished some years ago and replaced with a row of Identikit shops. Miss
Moore shared Aldin's passion for animals and, after watching him sketching at a dog show,
requested a portrait in oils of her Irish terrier. The plan was for Aldin to stay at the inn
for a week. In fact he remained in Leatherhead for six months, painting dogs and horses
and pedigree Jersey cattle on Miss Moore's farm, where she had converted a barn into
a studio especially for his use. A measure of his regard for her was Aldin's dedication
in perhaps his finest book, *Romance of the Road*: 'To Emily Moore, for three reasons. Firstly,
because she is a very charming old lady. Secondly, because for forty years she was the
hostess of that old coaching house, The Swan Inn, at Leatherhead. And lastly, that many,

A hackney cabriolet carries Mr and Mrs Raddle and
Mrs Cluppins to the offices of Mr Bardell. From
Pickwick Papers.

(*left*) John Gilpin, a little watercolour drawing completed when CA was eight years old and copied from Randolph Caldecott's book, which had been first published a few months earlier.

(*below*) Caldecott's version of John Gilpin's ride, engraved and printed by Edmund Evans. This was the most prominent illustration in the first two of the artist's Picture Book series (they were published annually in pairs over a period of eight years).

PLATE ONE

(*below*) *Three Jolly Huntsmen*. An early Aldin print and another theme obviously inspired by Caldecott, being an echo of his illustrations for the 1880 Picture Book, *Three Jovial Huntsmen*.

Admiration. Among the first of CA's pictures in the style that was to make his name. Dated 1897, it was issued as a print by Louis Meyer.

Full Cry, from *The Fallowfield Hunt*, the set of six prints which became famous on both sides of the Atlantic.

Cadbury's Cocoa. Among the best known of Aldin's posters, but not as forceful as his work for Colman's. In this case he was tied by instructions from the company, hence the 'chocolate box' result.

PLATE THREE

(*below*) *The Portsmouth Coach.* Coaching featured in many Aldin prints. This one is from a successful series depicting mail coaches on the main routes from London.

Lady Currie with her sons, Bill and Hamish, following the staghounds on Exmoor. Unusual because it is in oils, a medium CA rarely used. He described the moor as The Riding Playground of England.

PLATE FOUR

The Devon and Somerset crossing Badgworthy Water, Exmoor, in the 1920s. Pine trees and scrub oaks on the hills have changed this landscape, but it is still recognisable as Lorna Doone country near to Cloud Farm.

In the stables. A drawing typical of Aldin's early style.

many years ago she befriended and gave to a very shy and very red-headed youth his first commission; the result of which was the terribly bad picture which now hangs in her dining room.' When she was close to death, Emily Moore sent for Aldin and they spent an afternoon together, chatting about the old days. She left to him the 'terribly bad' oil painting, which he accepted with mixed feelings.

The months which Aldin spent as a student at Leatherhead were important to his whole career. For the first time he was working on his own, among animals and without any worries. It was also the first time he had stayed at an authentic coaching inn, which had its own cabs, flys and landaus. Among Miss Moore's prized possessions, Aldin noted, was a cream-coloured horse which had been given to her by Queen Victoria. (According to an article in *Apollo* magazine by William Fawcett, who had known him for some years, Aldin himself had a white Arab, presented to him by Queen Victoria, which he depicted as 'a first-flighter in Leicestershire'. Since no other reference to the 'white Arab' can be found, it is possible Fawcett confused this with the royal gift to Miss Moore.)

Labrador.

Hunting in the Shires (above) shows a typical thrusting field, all beautifully dressed and mounted whilst *Hunting outside the Shires* (below) shows a more rustic field, with the huntsman shouting to the motley followers to 'Hold hard' at a check. These two engravings after CA are his earliest hunting scenes to be used in a book and were completed when he was 22 years old and before his characteristic signature had fully developed.

Brains, The Hunter. From a series issued by Welbeck Publishing.

2

BOHEMIAN DAYS

Takin' the field! Glorious sound! Wot words can convey
anything 'alf so delightful?

If Aldin led a renaissance of sporting art, then the person who provided the impetus was Frank Calderon, a remarkable teacher, who later numbered Lionel Edwards and Alfred Munnings among his students. Calderon ran a school of animal anatomy and painting which in the summer season accommodated a group of budding artists amid the meadows and thatch of rural Sussex. Although only five years older than Aldin, Calderon had already acquired a formidable reputation as an animal artist. He had been exhibiting at the Royal Academy since the age of sixteen and had won the patronage of the Queen.

So keen was Calderon to instil in his pupils the need to paint from life that he arranged for cows, horses and a variety of livestock to be driven through central London to a studio which he used for his winter classes. But at his summer school in Midhurst there was no need for such eccentricities, for there were farms all around. The young men and women made detailed studies of animals in their natural environment and put the finishing touches to their pictures in the comfort of a huge barn, which served as a studio. Plaster casts of animals stood on tables in the studio and anatomical drawings were on the walls, but Calderon advised his pupils to be cautious in their study of anatomy, advice which Aldin accepted without reservation. Calderon stated, 'I do not believe it is either necessary or advantageous for an art student to dissect. He should think of his subject always as living, moving nature, and my own feeling is that the best way to study anatomy is to examine the living subject, and with sketch-book and pencil try to analyse the visible form. Let the student make clear pencil outlines or very slightly shaded drawings, indicating all the conspicuous features that attract his attention. Let him try to realise which are bone and which are muscle, which parts move and which parts are fixed, and then, with the aid of his anatomy book, let him try to understand what are those outstanding features which he has noticed.'

Much later, Aldin set out his own thoughts, in a letter to Bryan Bodington, a student at the Slade, who was the son of Will Bodington, huntsman to the Whaddon Chase: 'Your drawing is improving but you want to draw from nature (not memory) legs and feet,

Frank Calderon, a remarkable teacher who numbered Aldin, Lionel
Edwards and Alfred Munnings among the sporting artists who joined
his summer school.

(above) *Coursing*, by Calderon, from an engraving which shows his early influence on Aldin. (below) *Coursing*, an Aldin drawing published in *Black & White* magazine in 1899. The two couple of greyhounds by CA and Calderon might almost be mirror images.

in side view, front view and back view – both of hounds and horses. It would be a very good thing if you could get hold of a book on animal anatomy for artists. Stubbs's is the best one, but it is rather rare. You could always see a copy and make sketches from it at South Kensington Museum library . . . It is, of course, only the external muscles and tendons you want to know something about.'

Midhurst provided another landmark in Aldin's progression towards scarlet and MFH. In short, it was his ratcatcher phase. He had adapted a blacksmith's disused premises into a studio, and adjoining this was a pigsty in which the local butcher kennelled a ragtag pack of 'hounds'. It was with this mournful pack that Aldin had his initial experience of hunting, dressed in tweeds and a cloth cap and riding a borrowed carthorse. The quarry was any fox, hare or rabbit foolish or decrepit enough to stray into their path, but for the most part the wildlife of the area was safe, as the mangy hounds spent more time howling and scratching themselves than following a scent. There was a 'proper' pack nearby, the old Goodwood hounds, which Aldin followed on foot, and in the summer he went out with otter-hounds on the River Rother. Each evening he read all he could about hunting foxes, stags, hares and otters. And so, when he was nineteen, he happened upon *Handley Cross*, the Surtees classic, and the adventures of Jorrocks fitted precisely his own conception of hunting.

Those outings with the otter hounds may have helped to trigger the rheumatic fever which Aldin contracted for the third time in his life while at Midhurst and it gave him a 'jumpy' heart. (Later in life he developed rheumatoid arthritis, which again was not helped by his firm belief that an artist could give an accurate representation of a sporting scene only if he took a full part in the chase or shoot. One of Aldin's contemporaries, Thomas

'If a man's inclined for the chase, he'll ride a'most anything'. From *Jorrocks on 'Unting*.

Artists, professional and amateur, sketch London Zoo's new giraffe
(1895). Aldin was not the only one to use the animals as models for
African life illustrations.

The Ounce, otherwise known as a snow leopard. A drawing from CA's
zoo portfolio published in *Who's Who in the Zoo*.

Blinks, renowned for his portrayals of country life, subscribed to the same theory and
suffered a similar affliction. He was sure his rheumatism was due to diving repeatedly into
icy streams, fully clothed, to investigate otter holts.)

Aldin returned to his parents' home in London to recover from his illness, to celebrate
his twenty-first birthday and then to bombard the offices of magazines with drawings of
various happenings in the capital. His first published drawings appeared in such diverse
periodicals as *The Building News*, *The Graphic* and *Boy's Own Paper*. Those were the days
before the advent of photographs in magazines and newspapers and the editors relied on
artists for their illustrations of events ranging from dog shows and pantomimes to wars
and parliament. One of Aldin's regular haunts in his search for subjects was London Zoo,
with its seemingly infinite variety of wildlife, all conveniently caged, so an artist could
sketch and paint to his heart's content, and go back the following day to finish an animal's
portrait. G.D. Armour was another sporting artist who found the zoo a source of useful
material in his student days, when it was not nearly so well patronised, nor so organised,
as it is today. Aldin became friendly with a number of the Regent's Park inhabitants, such
as the gregarious chimpanzees and shy giraffes. An old wolf came to the bars of his cage
to be stroked and patted and a Samoyed dog and dingo in adjoining cages expected similar
treatment. Keepers also got to know the fledgling artist and took him to see baby animals
too young to be put on show. His zoo portfolio led, in 1894, to Aldin's first important
commission, to illustrate Kipling's Jungle stories in *The Pall Mall Budget* and, as it was
serialised, it provided him with an income for months.

(above) 'The lion sat down.' From a big game hunter's description of his first encounter with the King of the Jungle, published in *The Windsor Magazine*, 1895. (right) 'So close that I could distinguish the scintillating of his pupils . . .' Lion and hunter meet head-on.

Aldin's interest in ancient buildings and Georgian settings in the golden age of the stage-coach was encouraged by Dendy Sadler, who was born in 1854 and whose own outlook was moulded by the old-world habits of his family and friends. Sadler, who was Aldin's mentor and host on a number of painting expeditions, was famous for his interiors of stately homes and inns, detailed conversation pieces and mildly humorous monastic scenes. (A description of Sadler's output, written in 1905, could just as well apply to Aldin: 'Like the work of Randolph Caldecott, his art is both ingenious and suggestive, always kindly, agreeable, and amusing. It reveals a healthy, vigorous outlook on life, and as he has a perfect gusto of amusing, humanising intention, he may be taken as a most welcome contributor to the joy of the world.')

Aldin, in battered hat and wooden clogs and smoking his inevitable
pipe, relaxes at his Bedford Park, Chiswick, studio during his
Bohemian period.

Only One In It, and she's a lady. A full-page drawing for *The Illustrated Sporting & Dramatic News*.

Whenever he could, Aldin set off for the country, to the apple orchards and hop fields of Kent and the grasslands of the Shires, the latter further whetting his appetite for the hunting life. When working, he was happiest in his own company and would sit all day alone, painting animals or a time-worn building; but once he had put down his brushes and been given an audience, he was one of nature's ringmasters. During the 1890s Aldin rented a studio in the Chelsea artists' colony, where his perky manner, sense of humour and obvious talent made him a popular companion and he was often to be seen with Phil May and John Hassall, who became two of his greatest friends. He also met and married Marguerite (Rita) Morris, the daughter of a City furrier and they set up home in Bedford Park, Chiswick, an area frequented by 'the Bohemian brotherhood of the brush', as gossip writers called them. Aldin was then twenty-five years old and it was a year when he was at his most prolific as a contributor to the magazines. He was also being accepted as a book illustrator, using his zoo experience to provide four drawings for a volume called *Lion-Hunting in Somali-land*. This was followed, in the same year, by *A Year of Sport and Natural History*, a book to which Aldin contributed three illustrations, *Hunting in the Shires* and *Hunting Outside the Shires*, both completed in 1892; the third picture, *Coursing*, being dated 1893.

The last five years of the nineteenth century saw an explosion of activity among the artists of London and Paris, with paintings and posters and prints the like of which had not been seen before and have not been bettered since. The artists worked hard and played hard, and the decade was called 'the naughty nineties' with good reason. Familiar faces in Bedford Park included the artists W.B. Wollen, Lance Thackeray, Tom Browne and Dudley Hardy, in addition to May and Hassall. Savoyard Harry Lytton, the entertainer Walter Churcher and the showman C.B. Cochran were among others who enjoyed the artists' company.

Most of them joined in hilarious parties at Aldin's studio, sometimes at Dudley Hardy's in Ravenscourt Park, or Hassall's in Notting Hill. Often a theme would be chosen, such as Dickensian or Georgian evenings, or an indoor gymkhana; Harry Lytton would be persuaded to sing, but always the night ended in boisterous revelry. The high jinks, however, were an antidote to the hard work. Aldin recalled visiting Hardy's studio one Sunday, having heard his friend was preparing a painting for the Royal Academy, with the exhibition deadline fast approaching. Expecting a small painting, Aldin was astonished to see Hardy stripped to his vest, working like a maniac with palette knife and brush on a twelve-foot canvas. Hardy worked almost non-stop for two days and nights, and the painting hung in that year's Academy.

In Bedford Park, Aldin experimented with posters and prints, urged on by Hassall, Hardy and May. There was a stimulating rapport between the artists, perhaps because their styles and subjects were so different they did not see each other as competitors. Aldin, Hardy and May were among the founders, in 1898, of the London Sketch Club, the main object of which was to provide a weekly sketching session for members, followed by a supper with invited guests. The mood of their meetings can be gathered from an incident involving the same trio. A deed for the lease of their club required May's signature, but he refused to comply unless there was a solemn ceremony. Aldin, in the guise of a baron, knelt with the document and pen and ink in his hands; Hardy, armed with a huge imitation mace, stood guard, and May, in the role of King John, then signed his 'Magna Carta'.

Lenore van der Veer, who was sent by the prestigious magazine *The Studio* to visit the Sketch Club, wrote, 'There is Cecil Aldin, RBA, a man whose work is known from one end of the world to the other, known for its cleverness and its captivating sense of humour,

With the Bramham Moor. Captioned: *Portrait of a Gentleman Taking the Waters, a sketch near Harrogate*. CA contributed more than fifty equestrian drawings to *Punch* magazine, this one in January 1905.

for Aldin is unquestionably one of the chief exponents of modern humorous and sporting life . . . Some there are who assert that the mantle of Randolph Caldecott has fallen over Aldin's shoulders; but, if it has, it has taken on the Aldin personality so completely that the last vestige of its former wearer has gone, and gone for ever; for Aldin holds a place in the English mind and in the great public outside our gates, at once distinctly and deservedly personal, and while his humour helps to keep us going, his skill in line and action is a constant source of wonderment.'

Van der Veer went on to describe the club's Friday suppers and the bi-annual *conversazione*, where the emphasis was on feasting, song and smoke. 'You may sing a rollicking

Taking a fence, a drawing for *Land & Water Illustrated* showing a contrast in styles.

A Fall's a Hawful Thing. A pencil, ink and watercolour drawing for the Surtees classic, *Handley Cross.*
Illustrations for the book demonstrate CA's sense of fun and his affection for John Jorrocks.

PLATE FIVE

(*above*) *Bunkered!* From *Twelve Old English Sporting Pictures*, all strongly drawn and with bright, flat colour ideal for prints which were issued originally at two shillings each, unframed. (*below*) *Home*. Also from the Sporting Pictures set, this one being the finish of a race. Although labelled 'English', at least two had Scottish themes.

PLATE SIX

(*above*) *The Twelfth*. Another of the Sporting Pictures, showing a sportsman of Georgian times setting off with his retrievers on the first day of the shooting season. (*below*) 'I declare I forgot the cap.' Mr Pickwick and his companions prepare to take cover as Mr Winkle's gun misfires while rook-shooting. From *The Pickwick Papers*.

'Out for a Jolly,' from a watercolour impression by Snaffles of CA in a South Berks point-to-point, which the artist presented to Aldin, who used it as a frontispiece to his autobiography.

PLATE EIGHT

The Prince of Wales (Duke of Windsor) enjoying himself with The Pytchley. A plate from *Ratcatcher to Scarlet*, the original of which was bought by the Duchess and stayed with her until her death.

lay between the soup and fish courses, or you may smoke before the advent of joint, and you may even shy bread pellets at your neighbour, but you must not under any conditions be serious – this is the one great offence punishable by death at the hands of your friends.'

There was plenty of joie de vivre, but nothing frivolous, about their art, however. All were brilliant exponents of their chosen branches of the profession, as was shown every week by their two-hour sketches at the club. Horses, dogs and hounds invariably featured in Aldin's contributions; John Hassall, when lost for an idea, sketched his fellow members. Lionel Edwards, who joined the club later, painted at one of their sessions a watercolour of an old grey horse destined to be fed to hounds. Aldin had been elected a member of

Leading the Way. A lady braves the wire in a broken fence. Also for
Land & Water.

the Royal Society of British Artists in the same year as he helped to found the Sketch Club. He was also to be seen regularly at Savage Club dinners and meetings of the Chelsea Arts Club. An indication of the times was the lack of female company at any of these gatherings. More of a problem was the demon drink, which killed Phil May and ruined much of Hassall's life. During earlier research, I suggested that John Hassall had become 'morose and introspective' due to an experience as a special constable in the 1914-18 war, when he had been sent to the scene of a munitions factory disaster. His daughter wrote to me, 'Quite untrue. He was affected by the experience you mention but it would be better to say...This helped to worsen an existing drink problem.' Miss Hassall described the Bohemian set's behaviour as 'juvenile larking' and she added, 'Speaking entirely for myself, I used to be appalled by it, as it seemed so un-adult but each must live to his own taste. The great evening of the year at the London Sketch Club was the Tramps' Supper, when they all came as tramps and took infinite pains to horribilise themselves.'

It was from Bedford Park that Aldin first hacked on his own horse to a meet, the chosen pack being the West Surrey Staghounds, meeting on the outskirts of Esher. 'For this great day, I started by road to the meet, exactly like the renowned Mr Jorrocks of St Botolph's Lane, to hunt with a Surrey pack,' he wrote in 1934. 'I do not think there is any other hunting man now alive who has hunted, as I have, with some thirty different packs of hounds, who can state that he started his career in this way, and actually hacked from London to attend his first meet.'

In fact Lionel Edwards made a similar claim about a hack from Kensington to a meet at Esher, although in Edwards's case it was not his first outing and he got there to find the meet had been cancelled.

That first horse of Aldin's was an old grey polo pony called Sweetheart, which was given to him by E. Boyce Podmore, Master of the Vine, in exchange for a portrait of his son, Robert Buckley Podmore, dressed casually and mounted on a donkey. Robert, who died when he was fourteen, was then nine or ten years old and had his own pack of harriers. His brother, John H. Podmore, recalled Aldin staying with the family in 1901 and painting a portrait of Boyce Podmore cubhunting with The Vine. It was a competent but by no means great painting, showing the Master cheering hounds into covert, the main interest being that it was in oils and one of the largest paintings attempted by Aldin in that medium. John Podmore, when in his ninetieth year, told me Aldin's reference in his autobiography to a portrait of Sweetheart as the price of the pony was mistaken. 'Bob did not hunt his pack dressed like this,' said Mr Podmore, in reference to the bartered picture. 'He had a roan pony, which lived for over thirty years and died a fortnight after my father died. Bob was the first boy to wear a huntsman's cap and he was always perfectly dressed as a huntsman.'

An interviewer who met 'the famous young artist' of Bedford Park, was intrigued by

Robert Buckley Podmore, known as The Amazing Master Bob, a picture
which Aldin swapped for his first 'hunter,' a polo pony called
Sweetheart.

a large stuffed horse, a bay mare called Sweet Nancy, which stood in an alcove of the studio and on which Dudley Aldin, who was then two years old, had his first riding lessons. In a shaded corner sat a full-size wax model of a woman, called Miss Smith, deliberately placed to startle visitors. Apart from the stuffed and waxen inhabitants, the Aldins' household had swelled to encompass the Podmore pony, a donkey, a black Shetland, two children and a dozen dogs or so. To this menage Cecil added his first real hunter, again in exchange for a painting, but this time from the Master of the West Surrey. The hunter was called Daddy, described by Aldin as 'a seventeen-hand chestnut gelding with a mouth like iron. As I rode about ten stone seven pounds I had a pound or two in hand, but he was a fine pattern, and although a bit over at the knee, a wonderful performer.'

Galant, a rough pencil sketch of a Pytchley hound.

44

3

HUNTING
CORRESPONDENT

All sheer 'unting – no nasty, jealous stipple chase ridin',
'urryin' 'ounds a mile beyond the scent.

Hunting fever had taken a firm grip on Aldin's life yet he could not explain why. None of his immediate family had connections with hunting, although they had always had horses and carriages and dogs. His father was a speculative builder who followed his own father in a business which at one time employed more than four hundred men. Nor could the blame for the malady be placed on Cecil's wife, who endured his hunting escapades with commendable stoicism. She it was who held the purse strings and endeavoured to balance the budget while her husband showed disdain for any suggestions that he should be accumulating investments and a bank balance. His attitude, often expressed, was that he was perfectly happy if he had sufficient money to hunt and to have a few dogs and to keep his family in reasonable comfort.

Even that modest ambition required much burning of midnight oil, for there was no inherited wealth to cushion the lives of Cecil and his brothers. The fortune their grandfather had made from the building of grandiose houses in the Cromwell Road area of Kensington had dissipated by the time of their father's death. Fortunately, the opportunities for a talented, hard-working artist were boundless, if ill-paid.

The practical experience which Aldin gained, little by little, in the hunting field and through carriage driving was being translated into prints and magazine illustrations. He had connections with at least five publishers of prints. One of the first to encourage him was Louis Meyer, for whom Aldin produced the forerunner of a type of hunting picture which made him a household name. This showed a huntsman, with hounds, giving the glad eye to a pair of modestly blushing damsels, while a cur-dog slunk away in the background. The treatment was bold, the subject mildly humorous and the huntsman's coat was picked out in bright, flat red. About the same time, Aldin delivered to Meyer a pair of carriage drawings, *Hyde Park* and *Brighton Front*, the latter showing Rita Aldin with two horses in tandem and her borzoi loping alongside. Dated 1897, they were issued as prints two years later. Thomas McLean was another publisher who valued Aldin's work. But the breakthrough into the mass market came when he was twenty-nine years old as

Brighton Front, a drawing which was issued as a print and showing Rita
Aldin driving, with her borzoi loping alongside.

'Dash my vig, wot men I've seen in
the 'unting field' – Mr Jorrocks.

a result of Lawrence and Bullen's decision to issue Aldin's series, *The Fallowfield Hunt*.

Lawrence and Bullen – later Lawrence and Jellicoe – had premises in Henrietta Street, Covent Garden, and their lists covered a wide range. The hand of A.H. Bullen, scholar and founder of the Shakespeare Head Press, can be seen in some of their selections, which included portraits after Bellini, Signorelli and Romney. The whole emphasis of their business was changed by Aldin and, to a lesser extent, John Hassall, and soon the work of these two artists formed the bulk of the company's output. 'Perhaps no series of pictures have ever quite achieved such a success as *The Fallowfield Hunt*,' exulted the publishers in their advertising literature. The Fallowfield, in a sequence of six, told the story of a hunting day: *The Hunt Breakfast at the Three Pigeons*; *Breaking Cover*; *Full Cry*; *A Check*; *The Death* and *The Hunt Supper*. In fact each picture had a tale to tell and their appeal

The Fallowfield: The Hunt Supper. Boisterous revelry in a Georgian setting, with a bowl of warm punch and a rousing chorus, in which the puppies join.

The Bluemarket Races: The Start. From the set of six prints which were designed for the same market as the popular Fallowfield Hunt.

was universal, which was why the sets were bought to grace hotels and country mansions and individual prints went to much more humble homes at a guinea (£1.05) apiece. Two characters who featured in many an Aldin print made appearances in the Fallowfield, a portly, perspiring sporting cleric and a boy on a donkey. Aldin's exuberant draughtsmanship, his bubbling good humour and his choice of Georgian settings caught the imagination of the general public on both sides of the Atlantic. So successful was the Fallowfield that Aldin sailed to the United States in an attempt to protect his copyrights from unscrupulous printers who were pirating his work. His English publishers were quick to capitalise on the demand for Aldin prints and produced another set of six, *The Bluemarket Races*, again showing incidents from a fanciful sporting occasion, with walking-on parts for the cleric and the boy on a donkey. In their catalogue, the publishers stated, 'The immediate success of Mr Cecil Aldin's now well-known series of sporting prints, *The Fallowfield Hunt*, encour-

The Bluemarket Races: The Finish. As with the Fallowfield, the pictures were full of
incident. They were issued at a guinea apiece.

aged the artist and publishers to produce an elaborate series of racing pictures of the early
part of the nineteenth century . . . these coloured pictures will appeal not only to sportsmen,
but to all lovers of fine drawing, rare humour and decorative quality.' A third set, *Twelve
Old English Sporting Pictures*, had an echo of William Nicholson's illustrations for *An Alman-
ack of Twelve Sports* of three years' earlier, but Aldin's very different treatment of his own
choice of subjects countered any suggestion of plagiarism.

Coaching was another theme which Aldin took up as a young man and returned to
time and again. As with hunting and racing, he believed there was no substitute for personal
experience. Whenever possible, he rode alongside the coachmen, making careful records
in his sketchbooks of the way they held their hands, of various items of equipment and
how the horses pulled. Often he would take the reins himself. He painted a number of
coaching pictures for various publishers before Lawrence and Jellicoe issued his *Six Old*

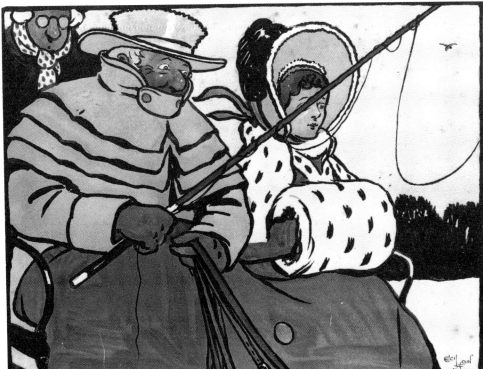

The Whip, a coaching theme in the *Old English Sporting Pictures* series.

Curling. Another of the *Old English Sporting Pictures*, although the subject is Scottish.

Coaching Roads in 1903, each showing an inn on one of the main roads out of London.

There seemed no end to the flood of Aldiniana to be seen in the shops, in the magazines and on the hoardings. No home appeared to be complete without at least one of his pictures and not only sporting themes, for some of his most popular designs were for the nursery, inspired by his children, Dudley and Gwendolen. The *Illustrated Mail*, in a fawning special article, noted that the Spanish Royal nurseries had been decorated with Aldin panels. 'The Queen herself selected the Cecil Aldin wallpapers that cover the walls of Baby's Flat. In the nursery, the little mite will be first introduced to the mysteries of Noah's Ark and all the funny animals. What Goosey, Goosey Gander did the baby will learn early from the wallpaper. In the same apartment . . . are coloured panels representing Hark, Hark, the Dogs do Bark, and Tom, the Piper's Son. The heir of Spain should soon learn his English nursery rhymes.'

Aldin was making regular forays with Home Counties packs, astride his first hunter, Daddy, and decided to try his luck as a magazine correspondent. He had already begun to contribute hunting jokes to *Punch*, although they preferred to call them 'humorous drawings'. He had also designed a new cover, a study of a huntsman, for the leading sporting periodical *Land & Water Illustrated*, which encouraged him to suggest that he should act

Cover design for *Land & Water*. The magazine first used Aldin covers in 1903, adding 'Illustrated' to its title and promising that photographs and drawings (many by CA) would form a prominent feature in future.

The Christmas Coach Crossing Marlborough Downs. An out-rider urges the
six-horse team through the knee-deep snow. Drawing on ivory paper,
heightened with bodycolour.

as the magazine's hunting correspondent for three guineas (£3.15p) a week. The editor snapped him up when Aldin added, 'I'll pay my own expenses.' He was to hunt one day each week and provide an illustrated article for the following week's issue. It was not much of a deal, as the payment did not cover even his travelling expenses, but at least it enabled him to hunt with a variety of packs, among them the South Berks – of which he was later to become Master – the Southdown, Garth, Old Berkeley, Surrey Union,

Aldin as Master of the South Berks. His appointment as MFH marked
the pinnacle of his hunting career.

A Little Misunderstanding. Punch, February 1905, captioned: Farmer (to
Young Snobley, whose horse has just kicked one of the hounds), 'I
should give the brute a good hiding for that, sir.' Snobley, whose
knowledge of hounds and hunting is only at present in embryo,
proceeds (as he thinks) to do it!

The Ups and Downs of the Southdown. A hunting correspondent drawing from a day
in Sussex, where steep downland contrasted with the pasture and plough of the
seaboard side.

Old Surrey, Berks and Bucks, West Surrey Staghounds and Ripley and Knaphill Harriers.

A trial article on cubhunting was a success, despite a near disaster for the prentice Nimrod, whose mount ran away with him, to the amusement of the rest of the field. Aldin had failed to appreciate that Daddy, a mighty handful for so light a rider, would answer his instincts as soon as he heard the huntsman's horn. He had been ridden for years by the Master and huntsman of the West Surrey and merely wanted to be with hounds as quickly as possible. Once he and Aldin reached an understanding they had three enjoyable seasons together. Aldin's regular 'Hunting from London' articles as *Land & Water*'s official correspondent began in January 1904 and his choice of pack for the first article was, significantly, his beloved South Berks.

Bedford Park, even in those days, would not be anyone's choice as a hunting centre,

The carted deer, a sketch for a Hunting From London article. Contrary to popular
belief, the deer was not harmed but was captured after a chase and taken away to
run another day.

and so Aldin moved to Henley, where he rented a large house with a walled garden on
what is now the site of the town's main post office. This was a period in which he was
extremely busy, providing a stream of marvellous illustrations for books, in addition to
his magazine work, his prints and a growing number of commissions. Whenever he could,
he stole a day with the South Berks, the Garth, or the Berks and Bucks Staghounds. This
meant rising at the crack of dawn to prepare for the day and, on his return in the evening,
a quick bath, dinner and several hours' drawing in the studio. He had also begun his summer
habit of spending a month or two on Exmoor, during which he went out with the Devon
and Somerset Staghounds.

An exhibition of his work in Paris gave Aldin the opportunity to meet a number of
French sportsmen, resulting in an invitation from the Compte de Vallons, Master of the
Forêt d'Halatte Staghounds, to spend a season hunting the forests of Lyons and d'Halatte.
Aldin was never an enthusiastic staghunter and the Frenchmen's long ceremony of dispos-
ing of the remains after the animal had been despatched with a pistol shot, was not to

A Likely Spot. The parson and the boy who featured in many an Aldin print indulge in a little fishing. Pen and watercolour drawing from *A Sporting Garland*. As with most Aldin pictures in this genre, there are deft touches of humour: frogs head for the water, a cat peers from the grass and a notice prohibits fishing.

PLATE NINE

The First Fence. An example of Aldin's rollicking depiction of hunting in the early nineteenth century, although this was one of a number of prints issued by Eyre & Spottiswoode in the 1920s and 1930s.

Preston Rawnsley of the Southwold, on Bluebird. A large pastel portrait ($38\frac{1}{2} \times 59$ in) presented to him in 1920 'in grateful recognition of the excellent sport shown by him as Master and Huntsman for forty years'. He rode Bluebird for twelve seasons. Hounds shown include Heedful, Artful, Decanter and Helen.

PLATE TEN

(above) *A Timber Topper with The Quorn*. One of four *Hunting Types* issued as prints, the others showing *A Warwickshire Thruster*, *A Pytchley Double-Oxer* and *The Duke of Beaufort's Stone Wall*.

PLATE ELEVEN

(right) *Not a Hunting Seat*, illustrating the wrong way over timber. A plate from *Scarlet to MFH*, in which CA passed on his own experiences in the hunting field.

In the woodland, also drawn for the *Land & Water* series in 1904.

A Forêt d'Halatte hound. Descended
from one of the oldest strains in France.

Huntsman of the Forêt d'Halatte staghounds. Note the circular horn and ancient uniform. Aldin took the opportunity afforded by his Paris exhibition to go out with a French pack.

his taste. He was intrigued, however, by the hunt's traditions, handed down from generation to generation. The servants wore uniforms dating back two centuries, with tricorn hats, button-back coats and boots that went over the knee. Most of the field, wore circular horns, slung over their left shoulders in the manner of Caldecott's *Three Jovial Huntsmen*, and used the instruments to signal a sight of the deer, the hounds, an attractive lady rider, or as a greeting to the Master. An Aldin sketch of one of the 'blue' hounds in the Forêt de Halatte pack shows it to have been not unlike the blue-mottled Chien de Gascogne, probably the oldest strain of hound in France and the forebear of many an English pack. At the time of Aldin's visit, a very fine pack of Gascony hounds was kept by Baron de Ruble, who had been breeding them for fifty years, and a number were brought from France to resuscitate the pack of that ancient hunt, the Holcombe Harriers. This type of hound was known to William of Normandy.

Aldin pursued his twin careers with equal vigour when he returned from his long 'working holiday' in France in 1908. The Harefield Harriers series of half a dozen scenes from a mythical hunting day was issued that year, he had plenty of work on hand from book publishers, and his prints became regular features of the *Illustrated Sporting & Dramatic News*. He also became even more active in the hunting field.

As a born organiser, it had been obvious since the time of his escapades with a butcher's woebegone pack at Midhurst that Aldin would not rest until he carried the horn himself. His chance came when he moved to a cottage at Satwell in Berkshire, where he had room for a studio, a place to kennel hounds and stables for his horses. Local farmers warmed to his suggestion that they should revive a defunct pack which had belonged to Sir Robert Hermon-Hodge (later Lord Wyfold). After one season with Lord Wyfold's eldest son in charge, Aldin took over as Master of the Peppard Farmers' Harriers, hunting two days a week. The cash for most of the hounds and his horses came from Aldin's own pocket, which he justified by pointing out that he would not have to go far to find subjects for his work. One of these subjects was an old hunter, bought at auction, which would hold a pose, with legs arranged on buckets in galloping or jumping positions, just as long as he had food within reach.

The esteem in which Aldin was held by the harrier followers led to embarrassing moments. He detested elaborate brooches and pins, yet they presented him with what he described as, 'a gold pin with a very large hare in diamonds fixed on it'. He put it away in drawer but was asked repeatedly why he was not wearing his presentation pin. 'At the next meet a very self-conscious M.H. appeared, half hidden behind this enormous monstrosity,' he explained later. 'Luckily, soon after the first hare was found a nice hairy fence presented itself and the pin, catching as it was bound to do in the overhanging twigs, disappeared for ever.'

Aldin rode polo ponies with the Peppard because they were more suited to the awkward wooded country. For fox-hunting, he acquired a five-year-old chestnut called Whisky, which he had ridden with the Forêt d'Halatte and which his host, M. Jacques Kulp, gave to him in exchange for a drawing of the horse. Whisky was said to have coronet trouble,

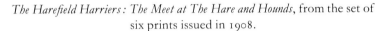

The Harefield Harriers: The Meet at The Hare and Hounds, from the set of
six prints issued in 1908.

Aldin, third from the left, as Master of the Peppard Farmers' Harriers. He carried
the horn with four types of hound, but claimed he had most fun with his
Peppard 'jelly dogs'.

but he carried Aldin after some of the most famous packs in the land without putting
a foot wrong for six years. This was when the artist was preparing his Hunting Countries
paintings, and went out with, among others, The Quorn, Cottesmore, Pytchley, Fernie,
Grafton, Belvoir, Duke of Beaufort's, Cheshire, Meynell, Atherstone, Devon and Somerset,
Fitzwilliam, Blackmore Vale, VWH (Cricklade), Whaddon, Warwickshire and York and
Ainsty.

Aldin's view of his undignified start as a hunting correspondent when Daddy, his first real hunter, ran away with him.

The young entry. Sketch for Hunting From London.

Easier Said Than Done. *Punch*, February 1905, captioned: Sixteen-stone
Sportsman (who has been nearly put down over a 'rotten' landing, to
Little Binks, 9st 2). 'Do you mind putting me back in the saddle, sir?'

4

THAT CHAP EDWARDS

'Unting is all that's worth living for . . . it's the sport of kings,
the image of war without its guilt,
and only five-and-twenty per cent of its danger

Hunting Countries set the seal on the acceptance of Aldin as an outstanding sporting artist and not merely a man who produced brilliant, but fanciful, prints. He was invited to stay with most of the leading foxhunters of the day and won their friendship and patronage, since few allowed him to leave their homes without at least one commission. The large paintings of each hunting country were also sold, more often than not to the Master of the hunt. It was time-consuming work and the amount of travelling involved forced Aldin to give up his harriers. In addition, the cost of transport, hotel rooms when he was not someone's guest, and stabling ensured he made very little money out of the pictures and the subsequent series of prints. He had the bonus, however, of enjoying the finest of fox-hunting country in the best of company.

Among those who invited him to stay was Lord Lonsdale, the sporting earl, a superb horseman, then Master of the Cottesmore and a former Master of the Quorn. Aldin was renowned for his control over horses and dogs, but he met his match in Lord Lonsdale, the sort of man who could quell a rebellion with a glance and yet was considerate to his guest's every need. The times he spent with the Cottesmore when Lord Lonsdale was the Master and Jimmy Finch the secretary, were among the highlights of Aldin's career.

While working on a hunting picture, Aldin would sketch members of the field from the saddle, making careful pencil notes of each rider's 'seat' and any peculiarities in their dress or posture. Particular attention was paid to the huntsman, the Master and any prominent followers. Hounds were watched at their work and in kennel; well-known coverts, fences, trees and other landmarks were examined and entered in the sketchbook. Later, Aldin went out alone, or with one companion, to study the landscape at his leisure. A common fault with some sporting artists, even one or two of repute, is a failure to portray a well-spread field of hunt followers in true perspective. Aldin overcame this problem by getting his companion to ride, or walk, to various points in the landscape, where he was halted by the artist's raised arm and further drawings were made, this time in more

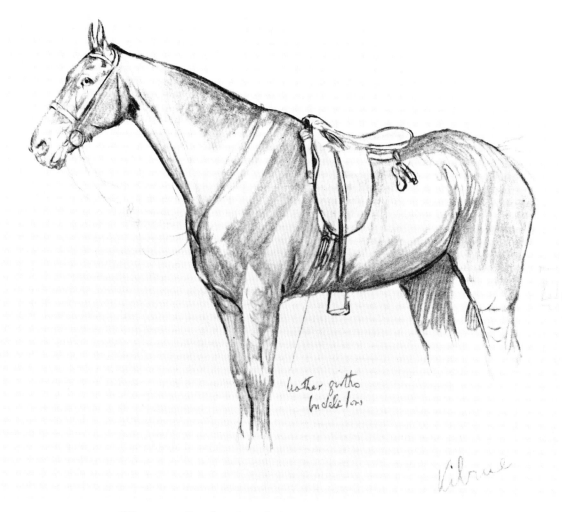

leather girths
bridle lom

Kilrue

Kilrue, a pencil and wash study for a portrait of Lord Lonsdale's hunter
when he was Master of the Cottesmore. Kilrue was brought over from
Ireland, where he won several races.

detail and with touches of watercolour. Then Aldin returned to his studio to complete
his painting. His attention to detail had, at least in part, a commercial motive. Members
of the field could be identified, whether they were to the fore, in the middle distance,
or background; and when the prints were published the first batch each had a key on
the back, naming the riders, which virtually guaranteed a sale to those named and possibly
also to their relatives and friends. Other followers bought the prints because they showed
so clearly hunting countries they knew and loved; and the general public bought them
simply because they liked them.

He was just as careful with his fanciful hunting scenes, which featured recognisable stretches of country and buildings. I am indebted to Captain Gordon Fergusson, keeper of the Cheshire Hunt archives, for the information that an inn shown in *The Cottesbrook Hunt* series 'is quite definitely the Swan Hotel, Tarporley, the headquarters of the Tarporley Hunt Club, founded in 1762'. Captain Fergusson, who is the Club's honorary secretary, also suggested a possible Cheshire connection with the fictional name of the hunt chosen by Aldin. 'There is in fact a village nearby called Cotebrook, so that could just have given him the idea of the name, being a play on the Cottesmore.' Another likely derivation is Cottesbrooke in the Pytchley country, familiar to Aldin from his days following that brilliant huntsman, Frank Freeman.

Aldin favoured watercolour for landscapes and hunting scenes, but he preferred to use pastel for portraits, which usually placed the subject in a well-remembered setting. For example, his pastel portrait of Preston Rawnsley showed the Master of the Southwold

A sketch from the saddle for *Hunting Countries*. This is the Cheshire, away from Peckforton Wood.

Mare and foal. A delicate drawing which may have been in preparation
for a larger work.

taking an habitual line on his hunter, Bluebird, with hounds all around and no-one else within a hundred yards. The artist was as painstaking with his portraits as with any of his other work. His pastel study of Lord Hillingdon, Master of the Grafton, involved his lordship in an uncomfortable few days. Lord Hillingdon posed for hours balanced on a saddle in the harness room and then, on his remarkable horse, The Sower, repeatedly jumped over a fence at Aldin's behest.

Another portrait, of the Duke of Windsor when he was Prince of Wales, was set in Pytchley country, with His Royal Highness looking debonair, his top hat at a rakish angle and mounted on a chestnut hunter called Forest Witch. The Duchess, who was then Mrs Wallis Simpson, bought the original from Aldin's son-in-law and it became one of her favourite portraits of her husband, perhaps reminding her of the day they met during a hunting weekend at Melton Mowbray. The picture was placed on a staircase wall at their home in Paris, where the Duchess saw it every day. It was still there when she died, and when the house's new owner opened it to scrutiny by journalists, who were impressed, but wrongly attributed the picture to Munnings.

Lord Annaly as Master of the Pytchley. Aldin rode many times behind Lord Annaly
and his famous huntsman, Frank Freeman. CA averred that the sporting aristocracy
were 'the most delightful companions anyone can hope to mix with'.

Kubbadar pulling and going in front.
From *Right Royal*.

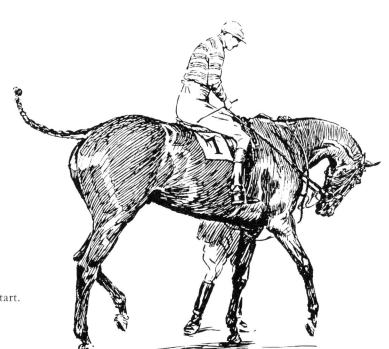

The big dark bay goes out for the start.
From *Right Royal*.

The superb quality of Aldin's commissioned portraits of equestrian subjects and dogs raises an inevitable question: just how good would he have been if he had chosen, or been able, to concentrate his talents on major paintings? His work paid for his sport, but with not much to spare, and so there were few times when he was able to put aside the cares of earning a living and produce a picture simply for the joy of it. That is the main reason he rarely used oils, due to the length of time it took to apply the paint, to wait for it to dry; to scratch out, to apply more paint and wait some more and to polish and to varnish and so on. He was painting for the day and not posterity, for a printer's deadline, for a veterinary or grocery bill, for the hire of a cottage on Exmoor. Only in the last ten years or so of his life did he have time to stand and stare, to enjoy the company of his grandchildren and his dogs; but by that time he had chronic heart trouble and was partially crippled by arthritis.

Another reason one is left with the firm opinion that he never realised his full potential was his compulsion, when he was at his most productive, constantly to change subjects. As a young man he was a bundle of nervous energy; wiry, pipe-smoking, never still for a moment, and the grasshopper in his nature was reflected in his art.

In his autobiography, *Time I Was Dead*, he remarked that he did not wish to plod along 'like Hogarth's industrious apprentice on those well-defined tramlines of art to which it has pleased God to call me'. He explained, later, '. . . all my drawing life I have tried to vary my subjects every few years. It is true that dogs and horses have been the staple dish, but sketching old inns, old manor houses, golf courses and even cathedrals, has made a welcome variety to my usual work. Like an actor who gets extremely tired of playing the same part for five hundred nights, I have always preferred to vary my occupation.'

To the above list he might have added drawings for around one hundred and fifty books, including some of the best children's books ever published, treatise on hunting and stage coaches, marvellous posters and so many illustrations for magazines it is well nigh impossible to trace them all.

Aldin's hunting scenes have been criticised for portraying some of the hounds and horses *ventre à terre*, as in pre-photography paintings. 'Has he not heard of Muybridge?' one critic was heard to mutter, in a reference to the sequence of action photographs of a racehorse

They're off and away to the first fence. From *Right Royal*.

In this caricature, John Hassall pokes gentle fun at 'Puppy' Aldin in their Bohemian days.

first published in 1887. Of course he had. No-one knew better than Aldin how hounds and horses placed their feet at full gallop, but he believed a modified 'rocking horse' effect, used judiciously, gave an impression of speed when he wished to portray a hunt in full flow after a screaming scent.

The depth of knowledge of some art 'experts' is exemplified by one who, in recent times, accused Aldin of plagiarising a John Hassall dog, a charge which would have sent Hassall into a paroxysm of laughter. The two friends fed one another ideas, but Hassall confessed time and again that he could not draw dogs and deferred to the expertise of 'Puppy' Aldin.

Comparisons have also been made between Aldin and Lionel Edwards. They were very different in character and in their approach to painting hunting countries. Edwards was tall, slim, courteous and deceptively languorous. Aldin was short, brisk, a no-nonsense

A hare goes down, and the retriever is away before he hits the ground. From *A Sporting Garland*, an oblong folio book and among the most attractive produced by Aldin.

Springer spaniels bounce through the undergrowth and raise a pheasant. From *A Sporting Garland*.

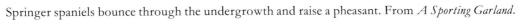

person who was at the same time generous to a fault. They knew one another from the Sketch Club days in London and Edwards had visited Aldin's Bedford Park studio, but they were never very close. The relationship was somewhat strained when Edwards began his own excursions into hunting countries. 'That chap Edwards,' Aldin asserted, was following him around and yet it was inevitable, as Edwards was eight years the younger and thus was making his own explorations that much later. And Aldin, it could be pointed out, had himself followed in the hoofprints of G.D. Giles's hunter. Aldin and Edwards, however, had in common a love for all animals and a deep knowledge of hunting, which shines from their pictures. Edwards also believed Munnings had never liked him, which may have been because Munnings and Aldin were good friends.

When it came to hunting scenes, the big difference between Aldin and Edwards was in the way the fields were portrayed. In Edwards's case, the atmosphere, the 'feel' of the hunt, was all-important. An oft-told story is of the man who went to an exhibition just to see the Lionel Edwards skies. It is no exaggeration, and Edwards's skies, sometimes taking the major part of his canvas, really do convey the mood of a hunting day. Aldin, with an eye on his prints market, concentrated on delineating the country and individual riders, with the sky providing a useful adjunct to a distant landmark.

CA with Lady Munnings on Exmoor.

(*above*) *Galloping Across the Map*. Aldin went to great lengths to ensure the accuracy of his coaching pictures, for which he used pastel, watercolour, and, occasionally, gouache. This one shows the Edinburgh Mail at full stretch.

PLATE TWELVE

(*below, left*) *Nell. A spaniel, retrieving a cock pheasant*. Pastel drawing used in the book *A Dozen Dogs or So*. (*below, right*) *Two Tortoiseshell Spaniels*, a type CA described as 'the most picturesque' he had painted. Their great feature, he said, was 'the deep, rich Belvoir tan markings over the eyes, cheek and feet'.

The South Berks. Aldin was connected with the hunt for about thirty years and became its secretary and Master. Here, with his friends, he shows himself, in black coat and cap jumping into a lane which marked the site of the old Roman road to Silchester. The huntsman, Isaac Sheffield, is with hounds, closely followed by Guy Hargreaves, MFH, and C. Eric Palmer. Behind them come G. P. Male, Captain Geoffrey H. Palmer, Miss Babs Rushbrooke, Alfred Palmer, Captain J. Figgis, Charles Rushbrooke, F. G. Lomax, Cecil Aldin, Mrs C. Eric Palmer, Mrs Harry Benyon, Sir William Mount, Mrs Geare, Charles G. Carter, Sir George Mowbray, Mrs Male, A. G. Henman (secretary), Miss Black, Charles H. Palmer, Lt General Sir Philip Chetwode, J. W. Hill, Lady Black, Miss Black, W. Mount, Howerd Dixon, M. Currie, Harry Benyon, Miss Keyser, Captain Beale, Major H. H. Edden, Major Maxwell, Graham Harding, Mrs Langford, C. E. Hewett, Captain Liddell, Lt Colonel R. Rees Mogg, Lt Colonel W. Peel Nash, Captain Noel Sutton, A. Targett, Miss Cory-Yeo, Captain Stirling, F. Vere Allfrey, Captain R. Mason, Oliver Dixon, Colonel W. L. Beales and Miss Sybil Keyser.

Mr Jorrocks and his hounds leave the kennels at the start of a hunting day. From *Jorrocks on 'Unting*.

'And they charged at the danger, and the danger took toll.' A pastel study used as an illustration for *Right Royal*, John Masefield's narrative poem about a steeplechase.

PLATE FOURTEEN

The Winner's Enclosure. Another illustration from *Right Royal*: 'To lead in the winner while the bookmakers cheered.'

Little Red Fox. From *Forty Fine Ladies*, sporting verse by
Patrick Chalmers (1930).

The Ladies' Kennel Association Show AD2000. Aldin was concerned about
the way physical defects were being bred into dogs to gain show points.
Here, at Christmas 1900, foxhounds appear to be excluded from his
ironic jest.

5

SCARLET TO MFH

'Untsmen are either 'eaven-born or hidiots – there's no medium

It was obvious to anyone who followed hounds that Cecil Aldin knew his hunting lore and methods. His knowledge was acquired the only logical way, through the kennel and the chase, supported by a close study of all the books on venery he could find, plus a ready ear for sensible advice, whether it came from a kennelman or an MFH. In Aldin's opinion, the three most important books for an aspiring foxhunter were Peter Beckford's *Thoughts on Hunting* (published in 1781), F.P. Delmé Radcliffe's *The Noble Science* (1839), and R.T. Vyner's *Notitia Venatica* (1847). Aldin believed a good grounding was the secret, with whatever type of hounds. I have Aldin's copy of *Foxes at Home*, by Colonel J.S. Talbot (1906), which contains much sensible advice and has passages heavily-marked in pencil, apparently by Aldin, relating to earths, cubs and ways of identifying the activities of dog foxes and vixens. Although he said he had more fun with his 'jelly dog' Peppard harriers than with any others, Aldin accepted they could not compare to the sport of fox-hunting with an established pack such as the South Berks.

'My dearest friends were made and my happiest years spent in the county of Berkshire,' he averred. The Palmer and Mount families were mainstays of the hunt and Seymour 'Doggy' Dubourg was the Master when Aldin first went out with them. The majority of members had known one another all their lives. They were a friendly, cheerful crowd, supplemented by officers from the Berkshire Regiment, who all kept hunters at the regimental depot. So far as Aldin was concerned, the tone was set when he was introduced to an apparently important member of the field, who was referred to as 'the official lubricator'. It turned out the man had in his pockets a number of flasks, which he pressed upon his riding companions at every lull in the day's sport, being most offended if they did not take a large draught. Aldin himself was a firm upholder of hunting traditions and so impressed the members that they asked him to take over as secretary, a position he quickly accepted. For several years, the Aldins had been living a nomadic life, but with Cecil's new position came stability in the form of a substantial house at the South Berks kennels at Purley, near Reading, which was to remain their home for two decades. Motorways,

The Garth in 1925. The huntsman, W. Daniels, is seen leading the way, closely followed by Reginald Palmer, with Prince Henry (Duke of Gloucester) between them in the background. Sir Herbert Cayzer, MFH, is clearing the fence by the tree. The field also included The Marquis of Downshire, Lord Dorchester, Sir Philip Chetwode and Sir Gerald Mildmay. In 1962, The Garth amalgamated with Aldin's South Berks because of the increase in built-up areas and new roads.

'Did you say two chests o' black and one o' green?' Mr Jorrocks, the sporting grocer of St Botolph's
Lane, pursues an order in the hunting field. From *Handley Cross*.

wire, housing estates and factories later changed the area almost beyond recognition, but
in Aldin's time the South Berks covered about seventeen miles square, surrounding Pangbourne and Reading and including part of southern Oxfordshire, with Henley-on-Thames
on the north side, Thatcham on the south, and split by the meandering Thames.

The boundaries had been unchanged since 1887 and were to remain so until 1962, when
the South Berks amalgamated with the Garth. According to *Baily's* it was bank and ditch
country; about one fourth pasture, the remainder being plough and woodland. A clever,
compact horse was recommended, 'one that can gallop and jump timber'. It was a country
Aldin was to know better than any other.

Even at that time a sporting magazine complained of 'veritable birdcages' in some hunting countries, although the South Berks had areas where a fair run was possible without
the hindrance of wire. There was another hazard, however, in the triple prongs of the
Great Western Railway, which spread from Reading like Neptune's trident. A run was
recorded during which the pack passed under a moving train without injury. Motorised
horseboxes were unheard of, so the entire field hacked to meets, up to fifteen miles, and
the horses' legs were hard as iron.

Describing the differences between hunting with a provincial pack and in the cream
of the shires, Aldin stated, 'In the Home Counties, perhaps, our huntsman is slower and

it is more necessary for him to *handle* his foxes than to give his field a series of gallops with plenty of jumping. If he doesn't catch his foxes the farmer will grumble, and the Master will grouse. He need not be the thruster he was in his youth, but the spirit to hunt and kill must be with him to the end. He must have untiring perseverance. Many of the field do not particularly want a fast hunt, they and their horses are not built for it, they prefer a slowish hunt with a kill at the end and a country with enough foxes and lots of gates. On the other hand, a slow hunt is a trying performance for a Midland huntsman, with a thrusting field behind him. I do not suggest that the thrusting division is not seen with provincial packs; they are always with us, and a thruster who cuts out the work over a trappy country, like some of the Home Counties, takes many more risks than the man who rides a good horse straight across Leicestershire; but there is always this slow division who enjoy the long slow hunts, which gives them plenty of time to make their little detours for open gateways, and still keep in touch with hounds.'

'Ar never gets off.' James Pigg flies a fence while Pomponius Ego holds back. Another illustration from *Handley Cross*.

The appearance in his first season as secretary of a handsome, two-volume edition of *Handley Cross*, lavishly illustrated with Aldin colour plates, gave a further boost to his popularity. It was his tribute to Surtees and the effort put into it demonstrated the depth of Aldin's gratitude to the creator of Jorrocks. He had given similar treatment to his other favourite book, *Pickwick Papers*, also published in two volumes with twenty-four beautiful full-page colour plates and many line drawings. In May 1914, with war clouds gathering, Aldin became at last a Master of Foxhounds, jointly with Eric Palmer, who soon had to hand over the reins completely to Aldin because of business commitments and preparations to join a cavalry regiment. It was due to Aldin's efforts that the South Berks pack survived the 1914–18 war. But he was unable to keep the horses together as by that time he had been appointed to provide mounts for the Army and the hunt's stables were not sacrosanct. He set up the first Remount Depot to be staffed by women and was helped in the work by his friend A.J.Munnings, before Munnings became an official war artist. Aldin was deeply affected by the terrible toll of the war, which wiped out or scarred in mind and body a whole generation of young men. His only son had joined the Army and on arrival in France as a subaltern with the Royal Engineers was sent straight to the front. Dudley Aldin was killed at Vimy Ridge, aged nineteen, while leading a company of Sappers, tunnelling between bomb craters to extend the trenches nearer to the German lines. Of the officers from the Berkshire Regiment who had ridden with the South Berks in pre-war days, only one returned.

At the end of 1918, Guy Hargreaves took over the South Berks Mastership from Aldin, who continued to live at the hunt kennels, where he converted an ex-Army hut into a studio. A large watercolour painted by Aldin in this period is of more than passing interest because it shows him hunting with his Berkshire friends, some of whom were associated with him for thirty years (see Plate 13).

Drawing used in *Scarlet to MFH* with the caption, 'A Peterborough hound is not always the best fox-catcher.'

Spaniels. A page from Aldin's sketchbook. He had more than 2,000 drawings carefully filed in his Purley studio, which he used for reference and never sold.

The Angler's Song, a chapter heading from *A Sporting Garland*, which covered hunting, shooting and fishing, with verses by Henry Fielding.

'In wintry woods, when leaves are dead, and hedges beam with berries red, the pheasant is my spoil.' *A Sporting Garland*.

The war changed Aldin's outlook on life and his artistic output. He hardly touched his pencils and paints for four years, but he did complete two wartime pictures, an interior of the Remount Depot and a girl ploughing, which were bought by the Imperial War Museum. He also made an unusual chalk drawing of an Avro two-seater biplane, in 1917, showing himself as a passenger being flown over Pangbourne and inscribed, 'Only half an hour's work!!' After the war, he at first concentrated on serious subjects: large pastel portraits of horses, dogs and hunting personalities. Children's books embellished with his work continued to be issued; there was a new series of prints of coaching houses and a book, *Old Inns*, but the illustrations had been completed some years earlier. The birth of his grandchildren, Tony and Ann, helped to revive his spirits and he resumed his working holidays in the West Country.

No matter where he went for the rest of the year, in peacetime, Aldin always reserved August and the first two weeks of September for his pilgrimage to Exmoor. He first discovered the area when a four-horse coach plied between Minehead and Lynton and passengers were greeted at Porlock by the village brass band. In those days, any sportsman who visited Exmoor headed for the Anchor Hotel, Porlock Weir, which was run by the eccentric John Goddard. The same group of people, from all over Britain, stayed at the Anchor each summer, taking their horses and dogs.

Aldin's routine was to go stag-hunting with the Devon and Somerset one day a week

Mr Jorrocks tries to 'get forward to the 'ounds.' From
Jorrocks on 'Unting.

in August, returning to Berkshire in mid-September for cubbing and to prepare for the start of fox-hunting. During two of the seasons he had a horse which was impossible to box and a groom took the horse and another hunter by road and under their own steam the one hundred and sixty miles to their Exmoor stable. The journey – which would be out of the question in today's traffic – did the horses good, according to Aldin. 'After all, twenty-five or thirty miles a day, with a long midday rest in a stable is nothing for a fit horse with a light weight on his back.'

When Goddard was mine host the Anchor was lit by oil lamps and there was a solitary bathroom, which caused a stampede of returning hunt followers each evening. But the guests loved the atmosphere. Goddard never advertised his hotel. He did not need to, for there was always someone waiting when one of the regulars dropped out. And what he lacked in business acumen was balanced by his wife. Once he had some port at 8s (40p) a bottle, but even at that price it was not popular with the guests. He was going to reduce the price, an idea his wife rejected. 'It's good wine priced too cheap,' she said. 'Put it up to 12s (60p) a bottle.' Goddard did as he was told – and cleared all his stock.

Aldin and his friends would be bitterly disappointed if they saw Porlock Weir as it is today, choked by cars and tourist knick-knacks and the Anchor updated and blowzily dressed in blushing pink, with the many sporting paintings which once hung on its walls replaced by cheap modern reproductions. They would, however, be quite at home in another of their watering holes, the Ship, at Porlock, outside which the villagers gathered morning and evening for the arrival of the coaches, heralded by horns and with the red coats of the drivers and guards flapping in the wind as they negotiated the frighteningly steep Porlock Hill. They would also approve the fine original sporting prints that still hang in the Ship, including Aldin's *Devon and Somerset*, with Porlock Bay in the background. Another familiar sight would be the wooden hut which Aldin used as a studio, on the road to Porlock Weir, and where he and Lionel Edwards held exhibitions of their work. Fortunately, the moor itself is little changed. The coombes and heather-carpeted slopes and the view over Porlock Bay remain as they are in paintings of a century ago. Cloutsham was one of Aldin's best loved places on the moor and he spent many an hour hacking, with his dogs running alongside and sometimes with his daughter and grandchildren for company. Often he would stop to record the view, perhaps from Webber's Post, Cloutsham Ball or Dunkery Beacon. When the hunt was out, he spent as much time sketching from the saddle as following hounds. He also made copious notes of the Exmoor tracks, to be included in a book about *The Riding Playground of England*.

Aldin's close friends, Denis and Kathleen Aldridge, shared his affection for Exmoor and they often went out together with the staghounds. Mr Aldridge, a former secretary of The Quorn and of the South Atherstone, was a fine horseman, one of the best to hounds. He was also a talented artist who helped Aldin during his Hunting Countries period. The

A polo match in progress at Dunster Lawns in 1924. Coloured chalks.

informality of the Devon and Somerset followers surprised Aldin when he first saw them, even though he had seen many drawings, such as those of John Charlton when he and Aldin worked for the *Illustrated London News*, showing men in bowlers, and even boaters, and lady riders carrying parasols. For them, the sporting event of the summer was not The Glorious Twelfth on the northern moors, but the opening meet of the Devon and Somerset at Cloutsham. On non-hunting days they had the best hacking country in England at their disposal, or they could watch or play polo at Allerford and, later, during polo week on the lawns below Dunster Castle. The Las Casas brothers were said to have played some of their best games at Allerford and the Indian princes were to be seen among the

Dull Polo!

By Cecil Aldin

SOME IMPRESSIONS OF THE FINAL MATCH BETWEEN
THE BRITISH AND AMERICAN ARMY TEAMS.

In the second chukka the brothers McCreery played a game of Aunt Sally with the goal posts while the American ponies, superior to ours in pace and agility, spun on their bandaged tails when their legs were otherwise employed.

These shots may look very very difficult but——

with a cute little martingale of Major Wilson's they are mere child's play.

Dull Polo! Impressions of a match between British and American Army teams in 1925.

Over the ditch, an
etching from Aldin's
later period.

visiting teams at Dunster, a scene recorded in watercolour by Aldin. In 1925, when the
Aldins and Aldridges were staying in the area, the Stoke Pero races were revived on the
moor, with some of the Newmarket polo team taking part.

Always an innovator, Aldin organised the first all-children's pony show and gymkhana,
which was held on a Cloutsham meadow, attended by about three hundred young riders.
He and his hunting friends devised a number of competitions which became a standard
part of gymkhanas and they repeated the event in following years at Dunster and Le
Touquet. Cecil Aldin was also responsible for starting comic dog shows and terrier racing,
inventing a contraption for pulling the mock hare which, with variations, is still being
used.

In the hunting field, he completed a unique quartet of appointments, becoming the only
sporting artist to have been a Master of Foxhounds and also to have carried the horn
with harriers, beagles and bassets. The harriers were his Peppard 'jelly dogs' and the foxhounds were, of course, the South Berks. The beagles formed a pack which Aldin collected
together during the 1914–18 war for cadets who were quartered at a flying school and
this became the start of a pack at RAF Cranwell. The first day out for those beagles, how-

CHAMPION
WALHAMPTON
MERRYMAN
KCSB 544 T

Champion Walhampton Merryman, the heavyweight basset. Aldin swapped this picture for
Godfrey Heseltine's stagecoach. In coloured chalks on linen, the original was large
enough (25 × 34 ins) to do justice to the subject.

ever, was a complete shambles. The Master and huntsman (Aldin) set off at a cracking
pace, only to find his 'field' of about three hundred cadets had stopped to pick blackberries.
They had been ordered to go out with beagles, but no-one had said they should run with
them. He had just as much fun with the bassets. They belonged to Godfrey Heseltine,
who went to India to hunt the Ootacamund Hounds and asked Aldin to look after the
pack. So he became joint Master with Tommy Carter and they hunted the bassets twice
a week for two seasons. Rita Aldin used to laugh uproariously at the sight of her middle-
aged husband in his green coat, white breeches and hunting cap, plodding after the lumber-
ing bassets.

During Godfrey Heseltine's absence Aldin painted a life-size portrait of a heavyweight
basset, Champion Merryman, which Mr Heseltine set his heart on owning. It happened
that the artist needed a coach to be used as a model and Heseltine, who had the very
thing, agreed to swap his coach for the painting. The vehicle was an enormous help to

Polo at Dunster. CA was a regular contributor of polo and general equestrian drawings to *English Life* magazine. This pastel was used as a cover illustration and shows a match in progress on Dunster Lawns in 1924, with the castle in the background.

PLATE FIFTEEN

PLATE SIXTEEN

The Grand National, The Canal Turn. One of a set of four scenes from the 1920 race, in which only five finished and the winner was Troytown. Aldin put himself in the picture, on the left, with his groom.

Quality. A showjumper being led away, proudly bearing a winner's rosette. One of four pastels from which a series of prints was made, the others being a hunter, polo pony and heavy horse.

A Meet at Le Touquet. Lithographic print. Aldin took his all-children's pony show to France in 1929, under the patronage of The Prince of Wales and with Lord Lonsdale as the show president.

Aldin when he was preparing his *Romance of the Road* book about the golden age of stage coaches. It was also used by the Aldins as a grandstand at race meetings, enabling Cecil to watch and sketch in peace, high above the milling crowd. They once took it to Epsom and parked it almost opposite the winning post to watch the Derby. Then came a deluge. The coach wheels settled immoveably in the mire and other coaches, cars, buses and bookies were packed behind it. Shortly before racing began, an official informed Aldin his vehicle was in a space reserved for a Royal coach which was due to arrive from Buckingham Palace. Aldin's offer of his coach for the Palace party's use did not need to be taken up because the rain persuaded them to cancel their visit.

The coach was stuck for three days, becoming a target for photographers and a playground for gipsy children camping with their families on the Downs. When ill-health forced Aldin to leave England for warmer climes, he sold his coach for £2. (The paintings for Aldin's two prints of *The Derby* and four of *The Grand National* had been completed before he acquired Heseltine's coach. In one of the National pictures he showed himself leaning on the rail, with his groom standing alongside.)

Romance of the Road, written and illustrated by Aldin, was set in 1828 and chronicled journeys by coach along the Bath Road and the Portsmouth Road out of London at a

The Grand National: The First Open Ditch. These set pieces lack the freedom and verve of most of Aldin's work, being rather lifeless and stylised.

His Majesty's Night Mail. Showing the four-horse team at full stretch,
with lanterns aglow.

time when George IV was on the throne, the Duke of Wellington was the Prime Minister,
and the Old London Bridge, albeit stripped of its houses, was still standing. The author
and artist used as his guides *Paterson's Roads* and the strip maps printed in *Cary's Survey*,
which gave the locations of 'gentlemen's seats', the principal inns and turnpike gates. Anec-
dotes about the inns and houses and their inhabitants are relayed in the book alongside
Aldin's own versions of the strip maps. He was unstinting in his admiration for the coachmen of long ago, citing as an example Charlie Holmes, who was given a memento for
driving mail coaches 598,000 miles in twenty-six years.

Aldin acknowledged his debt to James Pollard, Henry Alken and John F.Herring for
their paintings of the period and to Nimrod (J.C.Apperley) for his articles in the *Sporting
Magazine* and his essay on 'The Road'. Of Pollard, Aldin wrote, 'His horses may seem
to us a little stiff and conventional in movement; his coaches, to our modern mind, may
perhaps be too minute in detail, but to the student of the road every one of Pollard's
pictures tells a story, for they are pictures by a coachman and artist combined. Very high

artistic merit they may not have, but they hand down to us a story of horses, harness, travellers, mails, guards and coachmen, which no other limner of the period has been able to do.'

Herring, too, knew all about coaches and was at one time a professional coachman on the Lincoln to Wakefield run. Aldin commented, 'He is known more by his portraits of winners of the classic races and agricultural horse subjects than by his coaching pictures, but when we see a stage-coach painted by him we know that not a buckle or terret is misplaced.' Alken enjoyed greater renown for his hunting subjects rather than his coaching pictures, although, as Aldin remarks, 'To Alken the world is indebted for some delightful oil paintings of coaches by moonlight . . .'

In fact Aldin was himself no slouch when it came to painting coaches by moonlight, as he demonstrated in *Galloping Across the Map*, a wonderfully evocative picture, showing a four-horse team, at full stretch, pulling the Edinburgh mailcoach under a sliver of a moon and a starry sky, with the warm glow of lamps reflecting on the grey flanks of the nearside pair. By happy chance, the original of this picture is in the possession of his great-granddaughter.

Paterson and Cary were also useful to Aldin in the preparation of his book *Old Inns*

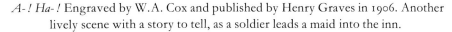

A-! Ha-! Engraved by W.A. Cox and published by Henry Graves in 1906. Another lively scene with a story to tell, as a soldier leads a maid into the inn.

The Edinburgh Coach. Aldin made a close study of coaching in the golden age.

and the several series of prints of inns and coaching houses. He had a great deal of pleasure over a long period from the inn pictures, especially as he usually managed to combine a visit to a country inn with a few days' hunting. *Old Inns* was dedicated to a famous fox-hunter, Lord Willoughby de Broke, 'because his ancestor's copy of *Paterson's Roads* gave inspiration for this volume'.

The eighteenth century coaching and hunting era inspired a stage show, 'The Good Old Days', written and produced by Oscar Asche, who persuaded Aldin to design the scenery and costumes and to provide horses, hounds and other animals. It was staged at The Gaiety Theatre, London, in 1925 but closed within two months, partly due to problems with the chorus and the death of Queen Alexandra, which plunged the nation into mourning.

Asche, famous for his record-breaking musical, 'Chu-Chin-Chow', wrote later, 'No play, thanks to Cecil Aldin's art and Joseph and Phil Harker's painting, has ever been so completely perfect as a production. It was a real slice out of the times. The real cobbled courtyard of the old coaching inn, the huntsman on his white horse, and members of the hunt in their pink and orange and blue coats, twelve-and-a-half couple of hounds, half a dozen

hunters, and the full-blooded life of those days.' Nine years earlier, Aldin had himself been the inspiration for a production at another London theatre, The Prince of Wales', starring a juvenile Noel Coward, Mimi Crawford and Fabia Drake. Entitled 'The Happy Family', it was described as 'Cecil Aldin Animals at Play.' Aldin's brother Arthur, a well-known theatrical manager, organised the whole thing. Knowing Cecil's love of Surtees and *Handley Cross*, he later attempted to stage 'a sporting comic opera in two acts' based on the adventures of Jorrocks. Cecil worked out a synopsis and Arthur pencilled in the cast, which included Berry Hale as John Jorrocks and two roles for Tom Walls, a fine actor and an enthusiastic field sportsman who had his own pack of draghounds and had often had days out with the Peppard Farmers' Harriers. The idea for a Surtees musical appears to have come from a couple of letters to *Horse and Hound*, suggesting that a film should be made of *Handley Cross*. But nothing came of it.

Arthur Aldin, who died in 1937, was very much involved in another pioneering film venture which did succeed in the early days of the cinema, putting the Grand National on the screen in London on the day of the race. He went to Aintree and travelled back with the film, which was developed on the train and then rushed round to a West End theatre. He did the same thing with other highlights of the sporting calendar, screening films within hours of the events. Arthur inherited the Aldin restlessness and in his time had been the manager of The Empire Theatre, Glasgow and a number of London theatres, including the Empire, Leicester Square and Daly's; he had been an hotel manager and printer, he had worked in Remounts and had been a member of the Volunteer Force in the 1914–18 war and he was in charge of arrangements for the VIPs at the Hotel Majestic, Paris, when Lloyd George stayed there for the Versailles peace conference.

Sending the Mail. Ink and watercolour drawing, dated 1902. A pair of
horses is unhitched and the mail gets through.

6

HELPING THE YOUNG ENTRY

Youngsters should be cautious 'o spurs – they may use them wot is called incontinently, and get into grief

Having carried the horn with four types of hounds, Aldin felt confident enough to pass on his knowledge to the up and coming generation in the form of two books. The first of these, *Ratcatcher to Scarlet*, stemmed from letters written to his son-in-law but which Aldin decided should be published, primarily for the benefit of his grandchildren and other young people. His observations, he explained, were not for old hounds, 'but we may also include the beginner in the noble art of fox-catching, of whatever age, be he youngster, subaltern, millionaire or embryo Jorrocks'. After steering the newcomer through the initial stages of buying and caring for a hunter, Aldin gets down to detailed advice, emphasising his points with drawings.

At a check: 'Don't chatter to the man next to you . . . See how quiet the huntsman is. Not a sound as he lets hounds make their own cast. The slightest noise now would get their heads up.'

In woodland: 'Never hesitate as to which side of a tree you are going, or your horse will hesitate as well and probably smash your knee.'

On jumping: 'Until you have had a little experience it is better not to take a line of your own.'

On kickers: 'Red-ribboned tails, the sign of a kicker, you must be careful about. People have been known to put this rogue's badge on a sheep, in order to get more room in gateway squashes – but you must not take any chances.'

On following: 'Never jump fences unless hounds are running . . . The farmer does not mind a smashed rail or flattened fence so much if hounds are hunting a fox.'

His other 'don'ts' included: Don't talk to a whipper-in or anyone else watching a ride. Don't grumble on a bad scenting day. Don't let go of a swinging gate until the man or woman behind you is ready to catch it. Don't holloa a fox away unless it is the only way to let the huntsman know. Don't turn your horse's tail towards hounds. Don't hesitate to jump off and open a gate for the Master or huntsman.

Leu-in, Leu-in! Used as a frontispiece to *Scarlet to MFH* (1933), CA's book of
hunting advice, dedicated 'To those good sportsmen who have much enthusiasm
but little money.'

Scarlet to MFH was intended to take the novice many steps further in his hunting career 'up to the time when he may himself contemplate taking over the mastership of a pack of foxhounds, harriers, or beagles'. The advice in this case included setting up a stable, hiring staff and keeping on good terms with various factions in the countryside, as well as the finer points of hunting hounds. Aldin made clear that traditional methods and ancient courtesies, dating back to the eighteenth century and beyond, still held good. They are just as relevant today, despite the great changes in society and in the landscape of many hunting countries. A major aggravation to him when hunting in his later years was the growth in the numbers of motoring followers. He advocated an instruction card to be placed on as many vehicles as possible, stating, 'Motorists are requested not to follow the hunt, as they head foxes, exterminate scent and disturb coverts by arriving at them before hounds. Subscribers' cars should never follow unless they have the permission of the Master.' He also proposed that those motorists who were given the Master's consent should keep behind a car marked with a red flag and driven by a hunting man who knew the country. 'They should stop whenever he does, and switch off engines at once.' That was written in 1933 and caused raised eyebrows then. It is not difficult to imagine how Aldin would react to the motorised chaos of the present day.

Aldin laboured long and hard to maintain standards in the hunting field, as witness his work for the Hunters' Improvement Society and the talks which he gave at many a social function. He was also a much better horseman than he would admit, describing himself as 'the world's worst point-to-point rider'. It is true he did not care for the victor's

Aldin's version of a selfish, fat-thighed plutocrat whose horses kick at everything within reach.

Hold hard! The Field Master shouting to the thrusters from behind. Also from *Scarlet to MFH*. Most of the illustrations for this book were in black chalk heightened with bodycolour.

spoils, but he did collect a number of trophies. When he won the South Berks Hunt Cup, however, it was in a year, he confessed, that he selected and marked the course himself. The following year he rode in every race, and fell in all of them. He would have won more races if he had not been reluctant to 'push' tired horses. Even when going well, a reminder to the horse could lead to problems, he found. 'I had just won the Hunt Cup and was riding a grey mare in the following event, belonging to a lady member of the South Berks Hunt. Naturally I may have been a little excited at having pulled off the previous race, knowing that I had a good chance in this one. There were only two of us in it when we jumped the last fence, and my mare seemed to have plenty in reserve for the gallop up the hill in the winning field, in fact I was a length ahead and felt very confident

Aldin learns his lesson the hard way, losing through unnecessary
use of the whip.

Aldin (left) riding, and leading, in his last point-to-point. Falls
aggravated the arthritis which plagued his final years.

of winning. Pride always comes before a fall, and I thought I would pick up my whip and leave my opponent a bad second.

'I squeezed the mare and she answered at once, but unluckily for me I also gave her a sharp but unnecessary reminder with my cutting whip, intending to demonstrate how good a finish I could make. She did just the opposite to what I had expected, for instead of increasing the pace and widening the distance between myself and the other rider, she just laid back her ears, "stopped", and landed her over-confident and stupid rider a bad second, when he could have won easily if he had left her alone.'

Falls at point-to-points and in the hunting field aggravated Aldin's arthritis, forcing him to stop racing and, eventually, to give up following hounds on horseback. His last two hunters, Oliver and Sausages, both had colourful pasts. Oliver had been bought in 1926 from a dealer, his third sale in a short time, and it was soon clear why. The horse was 'hot' with hounds and very nervous and was described as 'an excitable, fly-jumping brute'. When Oliver was tried in a hunt open point-to-point, Aldin was thrown heavily

CA's last hunter, Sausages, being ridden by Rex Green, Noel Sutton's stud groom.

The Huntsman. Copies of this panel hung in many homes. Children lulled themselves
to sleep counting the hounds' tails and trying to find the correct number of legs
to go with them.

and he arrived home in an ambulance, severely concussed. By dint of coaxing and petting
and trying out every kind of bit on the light-mouthed horse, Oliver's skittish disposition
was gradually overcome. An outing in Devon and Somerset country, galloping up
Dunkery, completed the treatment and Oliver became an ideal hunter, providing he was
not hemmed in.

Sausages was so called because he was saved from a French abbatoir and later bought
by Aldin, who believed the horse had been to the Saumur cavalry school. To the surprise
of his new master, Sausages could do figures of eight almost on a sixpence, leading off
with the correct leg on every change of direction. The two used to give dressage displays
at town meets while the field was waiting to move off. Sausages went to Major Noel Sutton
when Aldin could ride no more. Rex Green, Major Sutton's stud groom, said Sausages
was the fastest horse he ever rode. 'But he gave me more falls than any other hunter.
One day he would stand back and measure his jumps. Next time he'd skate right through
them, cutting them up by the roots.' Aldin, too, had a crashing fall while riding Sausages
and had to walk most of the way home because, being rather stiff in the joints and short
in the legs, he could not remount the seventeen-hands horse without assistance.

Well Over. Coloured chalks. The original was among a large collection
of Aldin's work sold at Sotheby's in 1977.

7

IS THERE ANOTHER?

'Unting fills my thoughts by day, and many a good run I have in my sleep

Increasingly crippled by arthritis, Aldin was advised to find a home in the sun and he chose the Balearic Islands. His horses stayed behind, but he took his dogs with him and had a studio built to his own design at Camp de Mar, Majorca. There he worked on his anecdotal memoirs and planned a book about Exmoor (which was published, posthumously, on a much more modest scale than he had envisaged).

He reflected on his life: 'From my first hunting correspondent bluff all my jobs have been experimental; I have appeared as an artist, play producer, scene painter, animal "property man", designer of nursery friezes, dog-fancier, remount officer, horseshow judge, comic or mongrel dog show inventor, toy designer, hunt secretary, MFH, Master of harriers, beagles and basset hounds, inventor of all-children's pony-shows, painter of golf courses, cathedrals and old inns and manor houses, maker of dry-point etchings and, my last experiment, designer of houses in Majorca.'

Hunting was never far from his thoughts, although the closest he got to hunting on the Balearics were terrier chases after lizards, which quickly disappeared up walls or into cracks between the rocks. On his occasional return visits to England, he spurned the idea of following hounds by car. He hesitated at copying a keen but incapacitated lady follower of the Cottesmore, who, clad in a mink coat, set off in a coster-barrow, pulled by a pony and was last seen at full gallop among the riders. He described his own preferred mode of transport for a crippled follower, 'A beautifully sprung Bath chair with waterproof hood set on a baby Austin chassis with no engine, a light pair of shafts, a smart trotting twelve-hand pony, and what more perfect and comfortable conveyance could you have for following hounds?' One of the nurses who looked after Aldin in the last few weeks of his life recalled that, even after a major heart attack, he retained 'his delicious sense of humour'. A portrait of a Pekinese dog hung over the bed and underneath the drawing he wrote, 'Once upon a time a lion fell in love with a squirrel. The situation was charming, but delicate. So the gods took pity. And the result was a Pekinese.' Mrs Gladys Elsmore (formerly Nurse Davies) told me, 'At that time I did not know he was a hunting man,

Sport on Majorca, where the locals shot any wildlife that moved.

but I now see why, when he became slightly delirious in his last days, he would keep singing "John Peel".'

After his death, at the London Clinic in January 1935, a memorial exhibition was held and some idea of Aldin's wide appeal can be gauged from the list of purchasers, who included old friends, such as the Palmer family, Lady Hunloke, Florence Nagle and Captain H. Tudor Crosthwaite; the author P.G. Wodehouse, and humorist Kenneth Bird (Fougasse of *Punch*); the Duchess of Bedford, the Countess of Stanhope, W.A. Cadbury and Sir Maurice Cassidy and dozens of admirers with addresses ranging from Berkeley, California, to Wellington, Somerset, and Lockerbie, Dumfriesshire.

Cecil Aldin would probably like to be remembered as he was just after the First World War, old enough to have achieved success and respect as an artist and MFH, and young enough to keep up with the pack. Patrick Chalmers, the author of four books illustrated by Aldin, recalled in a preface to the memorial exhibition catalogue, 'One November day in 1922 I was watching the South Berks hounds draw a big, hilly woodland. A lightly built, middle-aged man, reddish haired and very fair of complexion who, in a dark blue coat and velvet cap, rode a chestnut hunter, took my attention partly because of the grace of his horsemanship, partly because of an arresting gaiety of bearing which might have been that of a boy. 'Noticing my interest, a friend said, "That's our deputy-Master, Cecil Aldin." "The artist?" said I. "Is there another?" said he.'

Gone to Ground. The huntsman blows and a run ends in frustration.

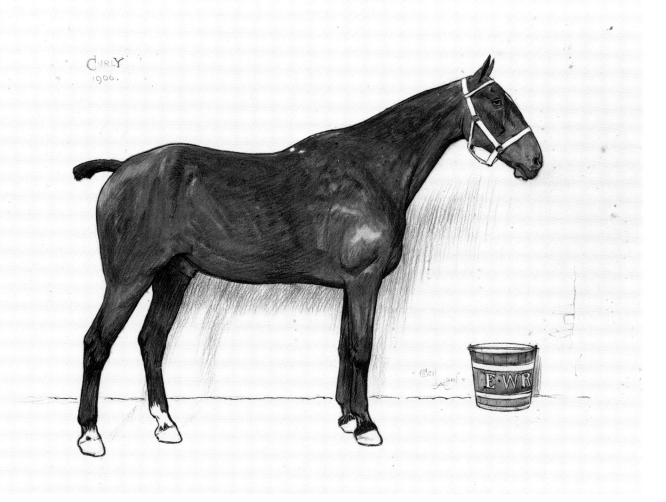

Curly, a fine watercolour dated 1906.

SPORTING BIBLIOGRAPHY

Cecil Aldin's career as an illustrator began when he was twenty years old, his first published drawing being of firedogs in a chimney corner at the Hollist Arms, Lodsworth, Sussex. Thereafter, until his death, not a year went by without new examples of his work being seen in periodicals, books, or in the form of prints which were popular on both sides of the Atlantic. He was one of a gifted band of illustrators who flowered in the late Victorian and the Edwardian eras, and, in his case, continued to flourish into the 1930s. Among their number were John Hassall, Phil May, Tom Browne and the Beggarstaff brothers (William Nicholson and James Pryde). None was as versatile, nor as prolific, as Aldin. The diversity of his output increased its attraction for collectors, but here a word of warning: the sporting prints have been widely pirated and there are also numerous 'Aldin originals' on the market which have not been touched by his hand. Many of these phoney 'originals' are easy to spot because of faulty construction and hesitancy of line, but others are clever forgeries. 'Hand coloured engravings' also need to be closely examined, because

The parson goes fishing and a black cat indicates his luck may be in.
From *A Sporting Garland*.

a large number are no more than tinted plates taken from books. As for the prints, the first to be pirated on any scale in Aldin's lifetime was *The Fallowfield Hunt*, mostly in America. Later, French and Belgian printers boosted their profits with unauthorised Aldin publications.

The quality of the original prints is obvious at a glance, in fact so good that some have been sold as watercolours. Many of the early prints were touched-up by hand, and when, as in a number of cases I have come across, the framer has cut off the publisher's imprint, both vendor and purchaser have been deceived. Some reprints, but by no means all, reproduce the first publisher's copyright imprint and the original date of issue where it can be seen at the edge of the picture image, while the new publisher's name is hidden by the mount, or the frame. Fortunately, the new frames, the smaller size and comparatively inferior quality of these reprints makes them unlikely to fool anyone. Another way in which purchasers of Aldiniana have been misled is in buying artefacts under the impression that they were made by Aldin personally, rather than to his design or in his style. For instance, his brother, Percy, engaged a number of employees who painted 'Cecil Aldin' horses and hounds which were cut out of wood, mounted on ebony bases, and sold at Ballard's shop in Reading. Early in his career, inspired by his children, Cecil Aldin designed and copyrighted four wooden animal cut-outs on rockers: a horse, dog, cat and cockerel. These were sold at leading stores in London and New York after the production was taken over by The Chiswick Art Workers' Guild. Aldin's coaching, hunting and animal designs were featured on tableware, including Royal Doulton.

After Aldin's death, prints and greetings cards were issued without regard to the copyrights. All the prints firms and most of the book publishers with which Aldin had dealings are defunct. Some had waived their rights in favour of his daughter. In 1960 all copyrights assigned by Aldin were returned to the family under a little known clause in the 1911 Copyright Act. In 1985 Aldin's work came out of copyright, under the fifty-year rule.

The following is intended as a general guide rather than a definitive list and includes only items with a sporting interest, as noted by Roy Heron.

Books with Cecil Aldin illustrations. Brackets indicate approximate dates:

1895: *A Year of Sport and Natural History*, edited by Oswald Crawford (Chapman & Hall). Three full page engravings after CA: *Hunting in the Shires*, dated 1892; *Hunting Outside the Shires*, dated 1892, and *Coursing*, dated 1893.

1895: *Lion-Hunting in Somali-land* by Captain C.J. Mellis (Chapman & Hall). Four b&w illustrations by CA, including frontispiece.

(1900): *The Horse That Jack Bought* by Howard Martin. (F. Frith & Co). Paperback folio-size book with full-page b&w line drawings.

(1900): *Roy's Wife* by G.J. Whyte-Melville (W.Thacker). Part of a 24-volume set of the author's works.

(1902): *A Sporting Garland* (Sands). A delightful oblong folio book with full page drawings of hunting, fishing and shooting.

1909: *Jorrocks on 'Unting* by R.S. Surtees. A pocket-size volume with three tipped-in colour plates.

PRECISELY as the clock was done striking seven, Mr. Jorrocks ascended the platform, attended by a few friends, and was received with loud cheers from the gentlemen, and the waving of handkerchiefs from the lady part of the audience. When the applause had subsided, Mr. Jorrocks advanced to the front of the platform, and thus addressed the audience :—

" Frinds and fellow-countrymen ! Lend me your ears. That's to say, listen to wot I'm

3

1910: *The Posthumous Papers of the Pickwick Club* by Charles Dickens (Chapman Hall/ Lawrence and Jellicoe). Two volumes. The 24 colour plates include coaching and shooting. One of CA's favourite books.

1912: *Handley Cross, or Mr Jorrocks's Hunt* by R.S. Surtees (Edward Arnold). CA's No.1 favourite. Also two volumes, with 24 colour plates.

1912: *White Ear and Peter, The Story of a Fox and a Fox Terrier* by Neils Heiberg (Macmillan).

1912: *Black Beauty* by Anna Sewell (Jarrold). Issued in various formats over many years (I have seven editions, all different, and there were others). The full colour plates include hunting and racing.

(1912): *Forager the Puppy* by May Byron (Frowde/Hodder). One of the Cecil Aldin's Happy Family series

1913: *Forager's Hunt Breakfast* by May Byron (Frowde/Hodder). One of the Cecil Aldin's Merry Party series.

1921: *Old Inns* (Heinemann). Text and illustrations by CA.

1922: *Right Royal* by John Masefield (Heinemann). Four marvellous colour plates and many b&w of steeplechasing.

1926: *Ratcatcher to Scarlet* (Eyre & Spottiswoode). CA's first book of hunting advice, for the novice, covering everything from buying a horse to tying a stock.

1927: *Dogs of Character* (Eyre & Spottiswoode/Scribner's). Mostly CA's own dogs, but includes French staghound and bassets.

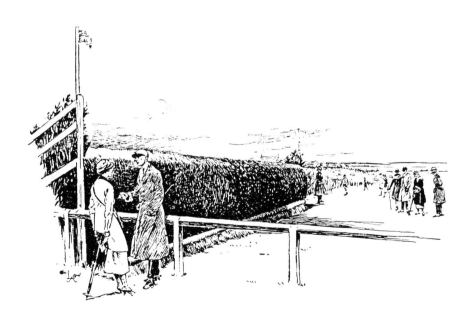

Golf by Henry Cotton. CA's cover designs were used for The Aldin
Series of sporting books (Eyre & Spottiswoode). The others were
Riding, *Hunting* and *Tennis*.

1928: *Romance of the Road* (Eyre & Spottiswoode/Scribner's). A handsome volume with marvellous colour plates and line drawings. CA's tribute to the golden age of coaching.

1928: *A Dozen Dogs or So* by Patrick Chalmers (Eyre & Spottiswoode/Scribners). Includes hounds, retrievers and terriers.

1928: *In My Opinion*, edited by W.E. Lyon (Constable). Includes a colour plate of a boy on a pony.

1930: *Forty Fine Ladies* by Patrick Chalmers (Eyre & Spottiswoode/Scribner's). Hunting verse with tinted line drawings.

1930: *An Artist's Models* (H.F. & G. Witherby). About CA's dog models, including King Edward VII's bassets, a Meynell Hunt terrier and tortoiseshell Spaniels.

1930: *Jerry, The Story of an Exmoor Pony* by Eleanor E. Helme and Nance Paul. (Eyre & Spottiswoode).

1930: *As the Hound Ran* edited by A. Henry Higginson (New York Press). Illustrations by Aldin and Lionel Edwards.

1930: *Foxhunting*, vol vii in The Lonsdale Library (Seeley, Service & Co). CA article on fox-hunting in the Home Counties with monochrome illustration of The Garth.

(1930): *Roads and Vagabonds* by Kenneth Hare (Eyre & Spottiswoode/Scribner's). About highway robbery in the coaching era.

(1930): *Old Coaching Roads and Their Successors* by Arthur Groom (Eyre & Spottiswoode for LMS Railway Co).

How to Get Into the Eleven. Title-piece for an article by the England batsman Jack Hobbs. From *The Cecil Aldin Book*.

Cover design for *Scarlet to MFH*.

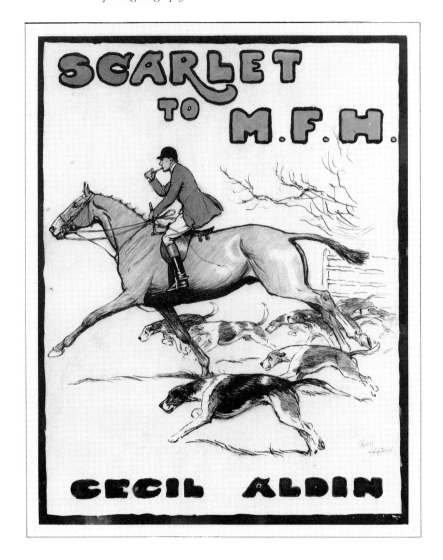

1931: *Riding* by CA and Lady Hunloke (Eyre & Spottiswoode). Advice for young people, with sketches by CA.

1932: *The Joker, and Jerry Again* by Eleanor E. Helme and Nance Paul (Eyre & Spottiswoode. Ponies on Exmoor.

1932: *Scarlet, Blue and Green* by Duncan Fife (Dorothy Atkinson) (Macmillan). Sporting verse with colour plates of fox-hunting, otter hunting and harriers.

1932: *The Cecil Aldin Book* (Eyre & Spottiswoode). Various authors but illustrated throughout by CA, including hunting and coaching plates, one being *Galloping Across the Map*.

1933: *Scarlet to MFH* (Eyre & Spottiswoode). CA's second book of hunting advice, for the improver, again with full page plates to support the text.

1933: *Dogs of Every Day* by Patrick Chalmers (Eyre & Spottiswoode). Verses about 12 breeds, including foxhounds, a spaniel and a Labrador

(1933): *The Care of the Greyhound* by Arthur Croxton Smith (Greyhound Racing Association). Coloured drawing of three greyhounds on cover.

1934: *Just Among Friends* (Eyre & Spottiswoode). Pages from CA's sketchbook including spaniels, a Labrador, borzoi and Ibiza hound.

1934: *Hotspur the Beagle* by John Vickerman (Constable),

1934: *Time I Was Dead, Pages From My Autobiography* (Eyre & Spottiswoode/Scribner's). Includes hunting reminiscences and sketches and Snaffles's portrait in colour of CA riding in a South Berks point-to-point.

1935: *Exmoor, The Riding Playground of England* (H.F. and G. Witherby). CA's tribute to his summer home,

1936: *Hunting Scenes* (Eyre & Spottiswoode). A lovely book, with some of CA's preliminary drawings of hunting countries, a foreword by his daughter and a description of each country by Sabretache (A.S.Barrow).

1949: *The Fox-Hunter's Bedside Book*, compiled by Lady Apsley, had a dustjacket design of foxhounds by CA and quotations from his *Ratcatcher to Scarlet*.

1981: *Cecil Aldin, The Story of a Sporting Artist*, by Roy Heron (Webb & Bower). The authorised biography, with many full-page colour plates and photographs covering the full range of CA's output and the first bibliography of his work.

Just Among Friends. Cover design for the American edition of the pages from CA's canine sketchbooks.

EXMOOR
*The Riding Playground
of England
by Cecil Aldin
With Sketches & Maps*

Exmoor. CA's tribute to The Riding Playground of England, published
after his death.

Periodicals with sporting illustrations by CA in his lifetime included:

The Illustrated London News
The English Illustrated Magazine
The Sketch
The Album
The Graphic
Punch
Land & Water Illustrated
The Windsor Magazine
Illustrated Sporting and Dramatic News
Pearson's Magazine

The Sphere
Cassell's Magazine
The Royal Magazine
English Life
The New York Times magazine
Black and White
Horse & Hound
The Gentlewoman
The Polo & Hunting Journal
The Pall Mall Budget

Little Binks Again. This is from the original drawing for *Punch*, November 1904, when it was captioned: Little Binks (facetiously, to Sportsman who is trying a new horse), 'You'd better send him back to the circus. That's his place.' Sportsman, 'He'd be all right, my boy, if he didn't see a clown right in front of him.'

Left the mail at the cross roads.   Met by John with the two new greys.

Made a good start.   But the wind rose and the snow fell.

And a drift proved too much for the two new greys.   However, with a scratch team from the next farm

The difficulty was overcome.   And he laughed with the lookers-on, pretending rather to like it.

TWO   NEW   GREYS!

Two New Greys. The young gentleman down from Oxford ends his
journey behind farmhorses after his spanking new ponies get
snowbound. From *Illustrated Sporting & Dramatic News.*

Advertising

CA designed a number of posters with sporting themes. One of the most famous – still being reproduced – was for Cadbury's Cocoa, showing a coaching scene. His advertising designs for Cadbury's included old-style golf in Scotland, two boys on ponies and others featuring rugby, cycling, rowing and cricket.

He made an advertisement for John Player & Sons with a coaching theme, to promote their Country Life Smoking Mixture.

Another coaching picture, *Behind Time*, was used to advertise beer for Truman, Hanbury, Buxton.

A drawing of hounds at a meet advertised Abdulla cigarettes.

One of his Old English Sporting Pictures, showing a tail-coated golfer, was used by Teacher's with the slogan, 'The Whisky of the Good old Days.'

In later years, he designed posters for his all-children's pony shows on Exmoor and for the International Horse Show at Olympia.

Love Me, Love My . . . Aldin provides a hunt setting in an advertising campaign which included the lines, 'Yet those old puppy days were too good to forget, with the scent of Abdulla – your loved cigarette.'

The Prints

Lawrence & Bullen/Lawrence & Jellicoe. Went out of existence in 1916. Many of the reprints from this publisher's range were much smaller, sometimes a quarter-size of the original issues.

'Straight' hunting prints:
1912-1913: *Twelve Hunting Countries.* Covering The Quorn, The Pytchley, The Belvoir, The Warwickshire, The Fitzwilliam, The Meynell, The Cheshire, The Duke of Beaufort's, The VWH (Cricklade), The York and Ainsty, The Blackmore Vale and The Devon and Somerset. A much re-issued series which was later extended to other hunting countries. The original prints had a picture surface of around 13x27inches (33x68.5cm), but the size varied slightly between subjects.

Fanciful sporting prints:
1899-1900: *The Fallowfield Hunt.* Set of six. 15x24½ins (38x62cm).
1901: *The Bluemarket Races.* Set of six. 15x24½ins (38x62cm).
1901: *Old English Sporting Pictures.* Set of 12. 10x12ins (25.5x33cm).
1903: *Six Old Coaching Roads.* 14x24ins (36x61cm).
1908: *The Harefield Harriers.* Set of six. 15x23½ins (38x60cm).
1914: *The Cottesbrook Hunt.* Set of Six. 14x26½ins (37x67.5cm).

Also: *Frank Freeman at Crick. Lord Annaly, MFH. Lord Lonsdale, MFH. Hunting Types,* set of four. *Horses and Their Riders,* set of six. *Show Jumpers,* a pair. *Riding,* a pair. Carriage scenes, including panels showing coaches on the best known mail runs. *Squire Brown,* a pair. *The First* (shooting). *A Likely Spot* (fishing). *Three Jolly Huntsmen. The Huntsman. The Whip. In the Open. Here's to the Hound. The Pick of the Litter. Jumping Powder. A Hunting Morning. The Old Huntsman's Farewell. The Young Huntsman's Goodbye. Drawn Blank. The Right Sort. Gone Away. A Check.*

Eyre & Spottiswoode. Absorbed into the Associated Book Publishers' group, but no longer publishes prints.

A series of 28 coaching inns. Mostly around 15x12ins (38x30.5cm).
Sporting and Coaching. Set of four. 9x15ins (23x38cm).
Famous Golf Links. Set of eight. 14x19ins (36x50cm).
The Prince of Wales With The Pytchley. 18x15½ins (46x39.5cm).

Walton Heath, the 17th. From the set of eight *Famous Golf Links*,
published by Eyre & Spottiswoode.

Richard Wyman. Defunct since 1950. Wyman published a number of Aldin sporting subjects in the 1920s. The most important were:

The Grand National. Set of four. 13¼x25ins (33.5x63.5cm).
The Derby. A pair. 14x19½ins (36x49.5cm).
New subjects were issued from The Cottesmore, The Atherstone, The South Dorset and The Grafton, all around 13x24ins (33x61cm).
Wyman also re-issued prints from Lawrence & Jellicoe's extensive range. These included some of the earlier Hunting Countries, but in smaller format, 6x11ins (15x30cm).

Alfred Bell. Now defunct. Hunting countries: The South Berks, The Garth and The Devon and Somerset. All around 13x24ins (33x61cm).

Aldin's friend, Denis Aldridge, published privately two hunting prints: *The Grafton* and *Lord Hillingdon* on The Sower.

Hunting, carriage and stagecoach prints were issued by Louis Meyer, Thomas McLean, Henry Graves, Welbeck Publishing and E.W.Savory.

Greyhound. A portrait on porcelain.

INDEX

References to illustrations are shown in *italics*